The Natural Garden

Natural gardening does not mean, as many people seem to think, that your garden must become an unruly wilderness of weeds. Far from it; it can be as neat as you like. What it does mean is learning to garden without chemicals. It is, ultimately, the art or science of gardening with nature instead of against it.

This book is not a subtle and subversive attempt to undermine the chemical manufacturing industries. Nor is it a banner-waving attempt to start an ecological revolution – though it might help in that direction. It is a book about gardening, and about gardening without poisons.

ROGER GROUNDS

The Natural Garden

MAGNUM BOOKS

Methuen Paperbacks Ltd

A Magnum Book

THE NATURAL GARDEN
ISBN 0 417 01920 3

First published in Great Britain 1976
by Davis-Poynter Ltd
Magnum edition published 1978

Copyright © 1976 by Roger Grounds

Magnum Books are published by
Methuen Paperbacks Ltd
11 New Fetter Lane, London EC4P 4EE

Made and printed in Great Britain by
Richard Clay (The Chaucer Press) Ltd
Bungay, Suffolk

For my
Mother and Father
who
first taught me
to appreciate the
natural world

Contents

Introduction

Natural gardening is not so much a technique, more an attitude of mind. It does not mean, as many people seem to think, that your garden must become an unruly wilderness of weeds. Far from it; it can be as neat as you like. What it does mean is learning to garden without chemicals – without pesticides, insecticides, miticides, fungicides and herbicides. It is, ultimately, the art or science of gardening with nature instead of against it.

This book is not a subtle and subversive attempt to undermine the chemical manufacturing industries, they are big enough to take care of themselves. Nor is it a banner-waving attempt to start an ecological revolution – though it might help in that direction. Every gardener who abandons chemicals and takes up natural gardening is improving the world he lives in. It is a book about gardening, and about gardening without poisons.

The problem, seen historically, is primarily one of attitudes. Ever since the agricultural revolution – when man stopped gathering nuts and berries and started cultivating his plants, his basic attitude to the bugs that afflict his plants has been the same, to bash, batter and poison them into submission. It is an attitude that does not work, that can never work. In spite of the sophisticated poisons available to us today, every year, taking an average over the last decade, fungus diseases in grain crops destroy enough food to feed 300,000,000 people. More than enough to save the lives of the 60,000,000 people who starve to death each year: unnecessarily.

Behind that attitude lies an even more fundamental one, the attitude that man is master of the world, lord of all he surveys and much that is too tiny for him to see with the naked eye. He sees nature as provided by some beneficent god to serve his every whim, to obey him and, like some servant wench, to be drubbed into submission to his every wish when she displeases him. It is a mediaeval, anthropocentric view of the world.

The reality is different. Nature is not there to serve man, nor man to serve nature. Both exist in the same world. The relationship is one of interdependence. Man is merely one of millions of species of plants and animals on earth caught up in the perpetual struggle for survival. For the present he seems to have become the dominant species: other species were dominant before him, and it may be that more successful species will succeed him.

Man has a lot of admirable qualities. He has industry, energy, imagination, curiosity and with these he has managed to evolve a technology, a wealth of information, far beyond that achieved by any other species. But we, in the industrio-technological nations of the western world, lack the most important quality of all. We are without wisdom. We imagine that because we invent something like DDT and seem to wipe out malaria over large areas of the world we have won a battle: we have not. We have lost it. There are now more than 750 species of insects which have produced mutants resistant to DDT. We invented a host of lethal chemicals to kill insects, and we have killed a great many insects, but again, we have lost, not won, because the mites, whose populations those insects kept under control, are now an even more serious and difficult problem than the insects which they have largely replaced, and we have had to develop even more deadly poisons to deal with the mites. So long as we look on chemicals as the ultimate solution to the problem of garden pests we are caught in a vicious spiral of having to produce ever more and more deadly poisons to keep up with ourselves.

If you want a garden in which every plant will thrive, in which the fruit and vegetables are wholesome and healthy to eat, there is only one answer, and that is to abandon chemicals and encourage nature to fight the battle against garden bugs for you. It will do it far more effectively than chemicals.

A simple explanation of how the natural world works illustrates very clearly just why natural gardening works, and why the modern chlorinated hydrocarbons and, to a lesser degree, the organo-phosphorus chemicals do so much harm.

All flesh is grass. The phrase is a simple one, and an ancient one, but it summarizes extraordinarily concisely the underlying facts of biological interrelationships. The word grass embraces all green plants, for green plants are the batteries which run the natural world. They have to be constantly recharged by energy from sunlight, and all energy in the biosphere (which includes all living organisms no matter how lowly or how highly evolved) comes from the sun. It is only green plants, however, that can convert that energy into biological energy. They do this by a process known as photosynthesis, whereby green cells known as chloroplasts in the leaves of plants use the energy from sunlight to convert water, hydrogen and minerals from the soil into complex organic compounds. In doing this they fix or bind that energy in a storable form, known as bonded energy. This is contained in substances such as sugar. If plants did not perform this process no other life could exist on earth. In the process of photosynthesis two types of molecules are formed, small ones and large ones typical of living, organic matter. Animals then eat the plants; they break down these large molecules and recombine them to form their own body tissues. In the process, however, some of that bonded energy is lost — mainly in the form of the heat needed to break down and recombine the large molecules. Animals that eat animals that have eaten plants again break down the large molecules of bonded energy in those animals and put them to use in building their own body tissues, with a further loss of energy in the form of heat. But the energy that is lost, and the energy that is bonded in those large molecules, is still the energy originally derived by plants from sunlight. This is simply the second law of thermodynamics at work: in essence that says that where any transference of energy occurs a certain amount of that energy will be degraded, dispersed and no longer available in a concentrated, useable form.

This biological system is known as a food chain. The plants are the primary producers: the plant eaters are the primary consumers, and the meat eaters are the secondary consumers. At each transference up the food chain as much as 90% of the energy available from the lower level is lost.

That is only the principle of the thing, and it may seem rather academic until you ramify the system into something more nearly approaching reality, and then lace it with DDT or some other chlorinated hydrocarbon. Let us take a concrete, well documented example. Clear Lake in California used to be one of the great fishing lakes in America. However, fishermen were troubled by a midge known as the Clear Lake 'gnat'. In the late summer of 1949 a programme of DDD spraying (DDD is a slightly less toxic form of DDT) was initiated to get rid of this 'gnat'. The application was at the rate of 0.02 parts per million (ppm). Within two weeks of the spraying no trace of the DDD could be found in the waters of the lake, and it was, therefore, assumed that all was well. The spraying eliminated about 99% of the midge. A further spraying programme was carried out in 1954, and the last in 1957 – by which time the midge and 150 other species of insects had developed immunity to DDD. Two weeks after each spraying the water was tested and no trace of DDD could be found in it. It seemed as pure as though it had never been sprayed.

There was, in fact, no DDD in the water. It had all been absorbed by creatures living in the water. The water is, in a sense, inert: the creatures living in it act as biological filters for substances entering the water. The lake was famous for the grebes which nested there and after the 1954 and 1957 sprayings large numbers died. An investigation was made into the cause. It was found that the microscopic plankton, the primary feeders, contained about 250 times the original concentration of DDD. The sunfish, which were the primary feeders on the plankton, contained about 12,000 times the original concentration. The grebes contained about 80,000 times the original concentration. That is working up the scale from primary feeders to secondary feeders and then up to tertiary feeders. The increased concentration of DDD at each feeding level is striking.

The mechanism of this increase in concentration is simple. At each step up the food chain nearly 90% of the bonded energy is degraded. By contrast, there is practically no loss of the DDD, DDT or any other chlorinated hydrocarbon. The poison becomes more concentrated at each step up the food chain, including man. It is stored mainly in the fatty tissues of the body; the kidneys, liver, testicles, mammary glands. The concentration of DDT in a mother's milk is even higher than that in her body. There are young women in America today, apparently perfectly healthy, who breast feed their children with milk that contains concentrations of DDT far higher than that permissible in cow's milk.

Apply this principle to a simplified ecosystem more like that of a garden, and the consequences of using chemicals in the garden become obvious. Take a system where blackbirds eat crickets which eat plants. Kill all the blackbirds. The first consequence would be a plague of crickets. There are no blackbirds to eat them. The cricket population, unchecked, would then explode and they would eat all the plants. That is about as far as most gardeners are interested in this food chain. Looking at a wider horizon the implications are horrific. The crickets, having eaten all the plants, would then die, and where there had once been a relatively stable ecosystem there would be a sterile world.

When a gardener reaches for an aerosol of some chlorinated hydrocarbon, it is exactly this sort of situation that he is creating. Insecticides destroy enormous numbers of insects: but the mites upon which many of the insects feed, have now become an even more difficult problem to deal with. Herbicides not only kill weeds, they also kill many beneficial insects that live on them and prey on garden pests. All too often the herbicides kill earthworms, with a seriously damaging effect on soil structure: many birds that eat poisoned worms also die, and they, too, keep pests down. When you reach for an aerosol, you don't just kill the aphid or caterpillar at which you aim it: you destroy a whole interrelated spectrum of the populations in your garden.

It really does seem incredible, and crazy, that if you want arsenic to poison the rats in your cellar you have to sign a poison register, yet you can walk into any garden centre and buy, off the shelf, poison fifteen times or more as poisonous. Make no mistake: there is no such thing as a safe poison, whatever the label on the can says. It is worth remembering too, that modern pesticides are brain-children of the Second World War. They were developed originally as nerve gases. They were meant to kill people, not pests.

You use them at your peril, and not just at your peril, but at your children's peril and your children's children's peril, because no one knows yet how long these poisons last in the soil, or how long they remain in the biocycle. All that is known is that they are very, very slow to degrade. There is even a suspicion that as they degrade they may turn into something even more lethal – but that is not proven.

You may well wonder, if all the resources of modern technology, chemistry and molecular biology, backed by the enormous financial resources of multi-million, multi-national chemical companies cannot solve the problem of garden pests and weeds, why on earth something as simple as not using poisons should work. Because work it does.

The reason is, in essence, just this. Complexity is necessary for stability in any association of plants, birds, animals and bugs. When you use poisons you simplify the system in your garden. Simple systems are unstable. In nature it is in the simple eco-systems that instability is most remarkable. In the arctic, for example, with relatively few species of plants and animals, there are violent fluctuations in populations. Some tiny change in climate will lead to population explosions in animals like lem-mings, foxes and hares. It is exactly like taking the blackbird out of the simplified example cited above. This does not happen in complex ecosystems, such as those of temperate forests. The lem-ming, for example, may have only one predator: if that fails to breed adequately the lemming population gets out of control. In a temperate forest things are more stable because there is always more than one predator for any one creature. Besides, there is tremendous complexity in the plant population of the forest, so that if, for example, you have a bug that eats hickory or beech leaves, there are plenty of other plants between the hickories and beeches which it won't eat: this acts as a natural check. Further, those plants in between offer a breeding ground for the bugs that feed on the bugs that eat the leaves of the beeches or the hickories. In the natural garden what you want is complexity, not the simplicity the chemical solution seems to offer. You are seeking the widest possible range of plants, birds, animals, and insects. Each will contribute to controlling violent fluctuations in the popu-lation of species in any of the other groups.

If you stopped using poisons in your garden today, you could achieve that sort of stability within two years. The word stability is used deliberately in preference to the term 'balance of nature', though the latter phrase is often used. There is only a forever ongoing struggle for dominance between species, some of which make short-term gains one season, only to lose ground the follow-ing season, while gradual shifts in the relationships occur through the slow aeons of evolution. Unless man interferes and upsets the precarious stability.

In essence natural gardening is accepting that gardening is

natural, that if you cultivate plants you must expect to find a fairly complex insect life coexisting with it. It means accepting that in some years aphids may be more of a nuisance than in others, but that in the long run the natural predators of aphids will control their spread, if only you will desist from using poisons and let these natural predators get on with their work.

It means accepting too, that the fruits and vegetables in your garden will grow better, look better and taste better than they do when grown with the aid of chemicals, and accepting that your ornamental plants will grow better and flower better and that, overall, your garden will look and will really perform better on all fronts than those of people who garden with chemicals.

Part One / From the Ground Up

1/ The Living Soil

To non-gardeners, earth is just earth. After heavy rains it is inclined to assume a semi-liquefied form popularly known as mud. Under extremely dry, sun-baked conditions, it tends either to turn into something rather like badly-laid, discoloured concrete, or else turn to dust and blow in your face.

To a gardener, earth is what plants grow in. The success with which they grow will depend, more than anything else, upon the nature and structure of that soil. A plant with the best will in the world, can never be more healthy than the soil it grows in. Indeed, the whole object of cultivation should be to have a healthy plant growing in a healthy soil. That is the cornerstone of success in natural gardening. So much so that 'a healthy plant in a healthy soil' could really become an *aide-mémoire* to every natural gardener as to just what it is he is trying to achieve.

When you think about it, there are only two parts to a plant: the part above the ground and the part below the ground. The part above the ground concerns itself with a lot of interesting activities – like flowering and fruiting and so on – but the prime function of the above-ground part is to photosynthesize, since without photosynthesis no green plant can survive. However, all this above-ground activity is useless unless the plant can take up from a healthy soil all the essential chemicals it needs. The take-up of these essential nutrients is the function of the below-ground part: the roots.

Nearly all plants have two types of roots. They have coarse, usually brown, roots whose prime function is to anchor the plant in its growing station. And they have fine, usually white, feeding roots and rootlets, often as thin as hairs, frequently almost microscopic, and it is these with which the gardener is, or should be, most concerned. They are also the ones over which the gardener can exercise most influence. They find their way, with incredible cunning, through the particles which make up the soil, seeking out plant foods. In good soils, they will maximize the opportunities available to them, ramifying over enormous distances. The fine, feeding roots of a single mature rye plant have been found to have an average total daily increase of an incredible five kilometres a day growing under ideal soil conditions. Feeding roots, however, are extremely delicate. In coarse soils they can be damaged very easily. Rubbing themselves against coarse grit they can destroy their own growing tip: entering water-logged soils they die back, and other roots have to explore new soil to compensate for the loss. Extremely dry conditions will damage them in other ways, often irreparable. Any damage or set-back to these fine roots is a set-back to the whole plant: any set-back causes physiological deterioration of the plant; and that in turn gives fungi, bacteria and other pestilential agents a chance to enter the plant and ultimately disease or destroy it. Once that happens there is a temptation to use chemicals to solve the problem, kill the bugs, destroy the fungus or whatever: anathema to natural gardening. Get the soil right and it will automatically follow that almost everything else will come right.

This may sound very easy, until you think of planting a tree that will grow 30m/100ft tall, and whose roots will delve down some 5-10m/20-40ft, like an aspen or a sassafras in America or an oak or a beech in the United Kingdom. It is only its holding roots, its physical anchors into the earth, that go that deep. Over 80% of the roots that feed the plant will be in the top ½m (18in.) of soil. And that you can do something about. Easily.

However, before looking at just how you set about achieving this utopian healthy plant in its healthy utopian soil, it is worth taking a closer look at soil itself, at just what it is, and why it is the way it is. Armed with that information you should be able to work out your own soil type and how to improve it.

According to most people, and come to that, to most books

too, earth is made up of three ingredients: mineral particles, humus (which is decayed vegetable and animal remains), and micro-organisms. Actually, that is not the whole story. There are two other ingredients in soil absolutely essential to the growth of plants – air and water – but these are present between the other particles. If we deal with the basic three first the role of the other two will become much easier to understand, particularly in relation to just what you need to do to the soil to ensure healthy plant growth.

One very important thing of which you should never lose sight when trying to assess the individual contents of the soil mix in your garden is that none of them matters particularly in its own right. It is the way in which the ingredients are combined that matters. Take the basic three ingredients (mineral particles / humus / micro-organisms) by way of an extreme example: if you have pure mineral particles – pure sand, say, nothing will grow: you have no humus, consequently no micro-organic activity. If you have peat – which is an extreme form of pure humus, nothing will grow: you need mineral particles in the humus to create air gaps in which the micro-organisms can live. What you must always keep in mind are the inter-relationships between the various ingredients.

Mineral Particles.

These are the prime determinants of your soil type. The mineral particles have come into being as the direct result of the erosion of the rocks which form the hard surface of the earth's crust. These rocks have been split by sun and frost, ground by the action of glaciers, pulverized by wind and water, all breaking them into ever smaller and smaller particles. The character of your soil will have been determined mainly by the rocks from which those particles were eroded. Sandy soils frequently overlie sandstone formations. The soil, as it were, developed *in situ*. The same is often the case with limestone soils. Often, however, the basic mineral particle constituent may have come from a great distance. The coarse, gravelly soils at the northern rim of the Thames Valley Basin contain mineral particles, often inconveniently large, that, centuries ago, were carried hundreds of kilometres by glaciers and glaciation. These mineral particles are fundamentally different from the underlying rocks. Similarly, but more extremely, the mineral particles in the silt soils in the Mississippi Delta may have been carried, suspended in water, for over 4,830km/3,000 miles. They may have come from Utah or Dakota or any state with tributaries feeding the Mississippi.

The origin of the particles will largely determine their size – which in turn determines many of your other soil characteristics. It will also largely determine whether your soil is acid or alkaline. The chances are that if the mineral particles were eroded from sandstone, you will have an acid soil, if they were eroded from a limestone formation you will have an alkaline soil. There are other factors involved in acidity/alkalinity. I shall come back to them. Whatever their source, those mineral particles are extremely important to your plants. They are the prime source of the mineral salts which, in solution, are what plants feed on. The basic classification of your soil will depend upon the size of those particles. Nothing else – just their size. This may seem absurd since the particles on their own are useless, but the size of the particles determines the amount of humus present, and the amount of micro-organic activity – if any.

Basic Soil Types.

Gardeners in the temperate Northern Hemisphere tend to divide soils into three basic types – sands, clays and loams. The extremes here are the sands and the clays. Clay soils have mineral particles of 0.002mm or less in diameter (1mm = 0.039in). Sand soils have particles of between 0.25mm and 0.50mm. Loams though seemingly an intermediate state and often stated to be such are more precisely defined. They contain a third particle type – silt particles. These are between 0.002mm and 0.05mm. The United States Department of Agriculture specifically defines a clay soil as one in which more than 30% of the particles are 0.002mm or less; sands as soils in which 35% of the particles are between 0.10mm and 0.50mm in diameter; and loams as soils in which one third of the particles are clay, one third sand, and one third silt.

Each of these basic soil types has its own quite distinct characteristics. Clay soils are rich in plant foods but difficult to work. They are heavy, literally, to dig, to lift, to work. They become sticky and gummy when wet because the particles are so fine they stick together with a quite surprising tenacity. They also tend to be badly drained, the minute particles only allowing water to drain away very slowly. In hot weather clay soils tend to bake like bricks, and become about as unworkable as a highway surface. Sandy soils, on the other hand, normally drain extremely well, and are easy to work at all seasons. However, they tend to be poor in plant foods, because these are washed through and out of the soil by the rapid movement of water between the particles. In summer, such soils frequently dry out and become like dust. Loam soils combine the best of both extremes. All three types are potentially first-rate soils. Clays are reputed to be difficult to work: with natural gardening techniques they can rapidly be brought into good condition. Sandy soils, which are usually thought of as being easy to work, are deceptive: in fact considerable skill is needed to bring them to excellence. Loams, though the best types of soil to start with, need care if they are not to deteriorate.

Extreme Soil Types.

If you live on a clay, sand or loam soil, count yourself blessed. Many gardeners have to contend with worse evils. One of the worst evils being that they will have to work a lot harder to bring their soils into a condition in which plants can flourish. There are four extreme soil types. They are these.

Stony Soils. These, by definition, contain mineral particles over 2mm in diameter. The over 2mm part is most important. The particles can be an awful lot over 2mm. At worst they may be nothing more than great chunks of rock that have slid down a mountain-side. At best they may be the rounded pebbles typical of gravel.

Peat Soils. These occur primarily in areas of high rainfall and poor drainage. Once drained, they look good and they feel good, but at worst they will grow nothing. At best they will only grow a very small number of highly specialized peat-loving plants — the sort of plants which created the peat bog in the first place: like sphagnum moss. Peats are almost pure humus: excellent as a sponge but containing virtually no plant foods and no micro-organic activity.

Muck Soils. These occur in dried up boglands where there has been neither enough time nor sufficient plants for peat to form.

They have one thing in common with peat soils: virtually nothing will grow in them. They look barren and they are barren.

Gumbo or Adobe Soils.   These are found typically in the south-west and far west regions of the United States of America, in areas of very low rainfall. They are usually extremely alkaline. The real problem with them is that, although they are usually fairly rich in plant foods, these plant foods are not available to the plants because there is seldom sufficient moisture in the soil to make the foods available in the form of weak mineral salt solutions.

Although these extreme soil types may sound pretty daunting, they can all be made highly fertile. However, it takes work, but turning one of these rather barren soils into a healthy soil that will grow healthy plants can be very satisfying. Curiously, perhaps, natural gardening techniques can solve the problems of these soils rather better than the prescriptions dished out by the chemical whizz-kids.

Establishing Your Soil Type.
Now that you know the scientific criterion laid down for defining the type of soil on which you might be trying to garden, the problem remains as to whether you do or do not actually know what type of soil you live on. There is also the problem of whether it matters. It does matter. If you try to improve a clay soil, along the lines suggested for improving clay soils, and it turns out to have been a good loam, you'll make it worse, not better. So start by knowing your soil type, then set about improving it.

The simplest way of finding out what type of soil you have is to ask other people gardening close by you. Accept what they say with caution. Soils can vary quite appreciably over very small areas. Even in a garden of o.1ha/¼ acre you may find pockets of sand soil in what is otherwise basically a good loam soil. Where asking other people is really useful is if you live on an extreme soil type – adobe, peat, muck or stone. If you move into an area with one of these extreme soil types, fear not: everyone for miles around will tell you the bad news at the first possible opportunity. And you can easily cross check. Certain regions of most countries are notorious for being peat soils or adobe soils.

A somewhat more scientific method of determining your soil type is to take a handful of earth from four or five different parts of your garden, mix it thoroughly together in a bucket, add a table-spoonful to a tumbler or clear glass jar of clean water, stir it thoroughly, then leave it to settle. Do not even attempt to judge the results until some of the water is completely clear: that shows that settlement is complete. A visual check will show that the largest particles have settled to the bottom of the container, the next size above that, and the finest on top of that. Over that normally there will be a dark layer, which is mainly humus: with many soils a proportion of humus will also remain in suspension in the clear water, some of it floating on the surface. With good loam you should have layers of approximately equal depth of large particles, mid-size particles and fine particles, with a further layer of humus of about the same thickness above that. If you have only very fine particles, so fine they look like mud, without any coarse particles, you have got clay. If you have got what looks like sand, without any finer particles, you have got sand soil. Typically, with sand soil you will find a lot of lightweight debris suspended in the water.

A more scientific method still is to take your four or five soil samples, mix them well together, and again stir them into clean water. Then, while the particles are still in suspension in the stirred water, pass the mix through filters of the correct mesh size for determining silt, sand and clay particles. These filters can be bought from most laboratory equipment manufacturers. Pass the mix first through the finest filter, then the next size up, then the largest size. Allow each filtered section to dry, then weigh them. Proportional weights will give you a fairly accurate soil assessment. More accurate still is an assessment of the different particles by bulk – which is the correct way of assessing your soil. Instead of weighing the dried, filtered particles, tip them carefully into a very narrow, calibrated test-tube. It does not matter too much exactly in what units the test-tube is calibrated, so long as you use the same tube for measuring all the different particle sizes. Again, it is the comparative amounts of each particle size that determine your soil type.

Humus. Mineral particles are essential to soil structure, but on their own they are useless. They are as barren and beautiful as Hollywood's idea of the rolling golden sands of the Sahara. Before plants can grow you need to add humus.

Humus is usually described as decayed or decaying vegetable and animal matter. There is, however, a general misconception of the function of humus. It is not, in itself, a plant food. Micro-organisms can break it down into foodstuffs which plants can use, and it acts as a sponge, retaining in a state readily available to plants the mineral salts in solution which are the prime nutrients of all plants.

Perhaps the simplest way of explaining the identity and usefulness of humus is to look at the eternal cyclic rhythm of nature. A plant lives by extracting mineral salts in solution and water from the soil, and carbon dioxide from the air, and using the energy from sunlight to convert these simple minerals into highly complex organic substances from which it builds its cells. Every cell in all plants, therefore, contains energy derived from sunlight. $E = Mc^2$. The energy is converted into matter. When the plant, or part of the plant – even a leaf – dies, it falls to the soil, and is gradually broken down into smaller and smaller fragments by visible creatures – earthworms, ants, other insects. Eventually these fragments become mixed with the soil. Soil micro-organisms then feed on them, converting the matter in the dead plant parts back into energy with which they build their own body tissues. As they consume the dead plant parts, they excrete into the soil adding new waste products of their own metabolism. When they in their turn die and decompose, they add still other valuable nutrients to the soil, apart from themselves becoming humus.

Generally people tend to think of humus as great cartloads of farmyard manure, lashings of leaf-mould or mulches of compost. In fact, although all these substances contain humus, they are not humus. Humus is minute – microscopic – collections of brown and black colloidal (jelly-like) particles of organic origin. Because of this they tend to accumulate in soil, and release food to plants very slowly. Like clay, plant foods adhere very tightly to the surface of these particles. Unlike clay, which is composed of mineral particles, these organic colloidal particles, though they tend to accumulate in good soils, are overall beneficial to soil. In particular, they will cling to clay particles, ameliorating many of the more undesirable properties of clay.

The earthworm is often cited as an example of a soil-living organism that converts decayed vegetable matter into humus. Recent research has, however, established that earthworms do not produce humus, or at least not the minute colloidal particles described above. If you are an observant gardener, you have probably noticed earthworms pulling fallen leaves down into the soil. You have probably also noticed worm casts. There is no real reason why you should have connected the two, but they are connected. The earthworm chews up the leaf and then excretes, in the form of worm casts, a lot of partially digested fibres, together with fibres it cannot digest, all mixed together into a sort of flour of which inert soil particles are one of the constituents. What recent research has established is that this flour does not contain the colloidal particles typical of humus. Quite what the properties of this flour are, or what its role in soil health may be, has not been fully established. What has been established is that both the true colloidal humus and the earthworm-cast type of humus are essential to a healthy soil.

Micro-organisms. Once you add humus — even in its loosest sense of decayed or decaying vegetable matter to the soil you also add, whether you realize it or not, micro-organisms. What micro-organisms do is turn decayed or decaying vegetable matter into colloidal humus. The more vegetable matter you add the greater the number of micro-organisms. One boffin has calculated that in a fairly average fertile soil there may be upwards of 100,000 micro-organisms to each cubic centimetre. What is interesting about micro-organisms is that they thrive best under exactly the same conditions as the roots of plants. Like the roots of plants, they need both air and water in the soil, and they compete with the roots of plants for these. Again, like the roots of plants, they inhale oxygen and exhale carbon dioxide. In many cases, they also, compete directly for the same foods as the plants. All of this may sound like undesirable competition for the available nutrients: in fact, the competition is highly desirable and greatly to be encouraged providing everything else about the soil is right, since these micro-organisms do two very important things. First, they convert many substances into forms in which plants can make use of them; second, more important than the competition of micro-organisms for the food plants want, is the competition between themselves for the available foods. The end result of this competition is that where you have really active soil population — encouraged by plenty of organic matter — this competition prevents specialized plant disease organisms from becoming dominant. Both factors are essential to achieving the objective of healthy plants growing in a healthy soil.

The Other Two.

So far we have looked only at the three major constituents of soil about which most gardeners know something and most gardening books list as the ingredients of soil. Now we need to look a little deeper. Get everything right about your mineral particles, your humus content and theoretically your micro-organic activity, and still you will not be able to grow plants. They need two further vital substances – water and air. Without these, though everything else may be perfect for plant growth, nothing will grow.

Water. This theoretically colourless, odourless and flavourless substance is essential to all plant growth for many reasons. But two of these reasons are outstandingly important. The first is that plants can only absorb the minerals which are their foodstuffs in the form of weak solutions dissolved in water. The second is that all green plants need water in order to carry out the complex process of photosynthesis. Lack of water in the soil prevents the take-up of plant nutrients, and brings photosynthesis to a standstill. A superfluity of water in the soil, on the other hand, will literally, drown the roots of plants: they will suffocate, because the excess water will exclude the oxygen they also need in order to remain healthy. This still holds good for plants which grow in water or with their roots in water. Water lilies, for example, have special hollow tubes in their leaf-stalks and their roots which retain oxygen. Plants like the swamp cypress *Taxodium distichum* produce curious knee-like knobs above water level so that some part at least of the submerged roots can breathe, oxygenating the whole root system. Mangroves have curious structures which virtually amount to snorkel tubes through which they oxygenate their under-water root systems. These special adaptations, evolved through millions of years, emphasize just how important the presence of both air and water are to the roots of plants.

The water that is of importance to the growth of plants is held in the spaces of pores between the other particles in the soil. The smaller the particles the more tightly the water is held: drainage is slow. The larger the particles, the less tightly the water is held between the pores and the faster the drainage. Clays have fine particles and drain badly: sand soils have large particles and drain quickly. Stone soils retain practically no water between their particles. Particle size also affects the availability to plant roots of the water held between the particles. In, for example, clay soils, which have very fine pores between the soil particles, the water is held so tightly that plant roots cannot draw the water out of these pores. The water that is of use to plants is held in the larger and medium-sized soil pores.

It is rather imprecise to talk of soil pores as large, medium or small. Recent research carried out in the United Kingdom has provided some useful data here, though it is still not as precise as could be wished. What it has shown is that where you are draining a soil, water can only be released by drainage techniques from pores larger than 0.05mm. That pore size can, therefore, be regarded as a critical size. If you have no pores in your soil 0.05mm or larger, it will be virtually impossible to retain water in the soil. The ideal soil would contain approximately equal proportions of pores above this critical size, and below it. Those pores above the critical size would be free draining and allow for the free circulation of air in the soil, while those smaller would retain the water the plants need. Such a soil would be perfect for healthy soil and healthy plant growth. One important implication of this data, an implication which is easily deduced but equally easily overlooked, is that those pores which drain freely are the main air passages in the soil. If there are insufficient of them, although a soil may not appear to be waterlogged, it will nonetheless be badly aerated: such air as there is will rapidly become stale with detrimental effects firstly on soil micro-organisms, then on the plants themselves.

A further implication, which is not obvious, is that sandy soils, which are world renowned for their rapid draining properties, may in fact have such a high proportion of minute mineral particles that there are no pores or only very few of the critical size for drainage, with the result that, contrary to popular belief, many sand soils are very poorly drained and badly aerated.

Air. From what has already been said we know that plants need both air and water in the soil in order to thrive, and that the air can only occupy those pores in the soil which are not filled by water – pores of more than 0.05mm diameter. Water will push the air out of those pores, but air will not push the water out. Under conditions of heavy rainfall those pores normally filled with air become full of water. In well-drained soils this water moves rapidly through the pores, flushing them out as it does so, so that they quickly fill with air again. However, if it takes more than two or three days for the water to drain through the pores, the damage done to the roots of plants, especially annuals, can be irreparable.

It is worth looking more closely at just why it is so important that air is present in soil. The roots of plants need air in order to be able to breathe: so too, do the vital micro-organisms. Both compete for the available air, using it in the same way. Both are continually using up the oxygen in the air and exhaling carbon dioxide. Both, however, are damaged, as are most living organisms including *homo sapiens*, by highly concentrated build-ups of carbon dioxide, an extremely poisonous substance in large doses. While it has not yet been experimentally proved exactly how the air in the soil is kept pure enough for roots and micro-organisms to flourish, it is reasonable to assume that, where there are sufficient air passages of sufficient diameter, there is a continual interchange of oxygen and carbon dioxide through the soil pores.

Problems arise as soon as this interchange is interrupted. The moment the air pores become blocked – for example by rain-water – a carbon dioxide build-up begins. Such a build-up not only damages the roots directly, simply by poisoning them, it also produces a radical imbalance in the soil population. Some micro-organisms are far better adapted to living in high carbon dioxide concentrations than others. Unfortunately the great majority of these seem to be unspecialized plant disease micro-organisms. Under conditions of good soil aeration their population density relative to the population densities of other micro-organisms is such that they cannot become dominant: both types of organisms are competing for the same foodstuffs, and only a limited quantity is available for them. The unspecialized plant disease organisms normally feed off dead, decaying vegetable matter, usually dead roots and the discarded cells from root growing tips. The moment this precarious equilibrium is upset by a carbon dioxide build-up, these unspecialized plant disease organisms attack the weakened roots of the living plants. This further weakens the plants, and where such carbon dioxide build-ups occur over long periods, these diseases can quickly get a hold on a whole plant, making it susceptible to a host of other diseases.

It is in order to avoid problems of this type that it is of crucial importance to ensure good drainage in soils of all types. Good drainage can readily be equated with good aeration. A soil containing a minimum of 10% by volume of air is normally considered adequately aerated. The optimum may be a slightly higher percentage, but too high an air content in the soil could obviously lead to a shortage of available water to the plant roots.

Summary.

If you started reading this chapter thinking of soil as a completely dead, totally inert substance into which plants put their anchors, you should by now be aware of it as a highly complex inter-relationship of animal, vegetable and mineral matter. If the chapter has read somewhat like a lecture in the structural physics of soil, that may not be a bad thing because, in order to achieve this ambition of getting healthy plants growing in a healthy soil, the first thing you have got to do is get the physical structure of the soil right.

But before looking at the best ways of doing that we need first to look at what the plants themselves need from the soil. Because that is intimately related to the physical structure of the soil.

2 / What Plants Need From the Soil

People eat plants. But what do plants eat?

Plants take energy from sunlight and use it, together with water, to convert simple mineral salts absorbed by the roots into highly complex organic substances from which they build and repair their own living tissues.

The most important of all plant foods are, perhaps surprisingly, the ones that are least often mentioned. They are hydrogen, oxygen and carbon. Plants obtain these from the air and water available to their roots. You cannot actually feed plants neat hydrogen, oxygen and carbon. You will not find it pre-packed at your local garden centre. The only way you can make sure that the plants you grow get enough of these three vital foodstuffs is to make sure that they are growing in the best possible soil you can give them.

Apart from these the main foods of all green plants are minerals in the soil which the plants absorb through their roots in the form of very weak mineral salt solutions. A small number of these are extremely important to all plant growth. These are known as the macro-elements. There are literally dozens of other minerals which they use in minute quantities. These used to be called trace elements but are now more usually known as micro-elements.

Macro-elements.

By far the most important of all the major minerals utilized by a plant in its growth is calcium. Funnily enough, its importance is often overlooked because in most fertile soils it is present in abundant quantities. Calcium is used by plants to build their cell walls. It is calcium that forms the skeletons left behind when a giant saguaro cactus dies: it is calcium that makes lettuce leaves crisp, and calcium that reinforces the spines of many prickly-leaved plants. However, although calcium is usually present in soils in large quantities it is not always available to the plants. This happens especially on acid soils: the calcium is there, the plants just cannot use it. That is a matter of your soil pH – a subject I will come to shortly.

The three other universally recognized macro-elements are nitrogen, phosphorus and potassium. Green plants draw on all three of these very heavily. Nitrogen is perhaps the most important of the three. Its prime use to the plants is for growth. Apply soluble nitrogen round a fast-growing plant – say lettuce – and you will see its rate of growth accelerate literally within a couple of days. Potassium is used by plants for forming their flowers and setting their fruit. Phosphorus helps plants to come out the right colour. Different plants use these macro-elements in different proportions. Grow *Agapanthus praecox* in a nitrogen-rich soil and you will get lots of long, bright green leaves, but no flowers. Dose it with phosphorus and the leaves will be a darker green, but you still will not get flowers. Feed it and feed it with potassium and it will flower magnificiently.

Micro-elements.
These are used by plants in tiny quantities. There are literally dozens of them, and there is little point in listing them all. They number among them all sorts of rare and precious minerals and metals, like magnesium, boron, ceasium, platinum, and gold. All the mineral plants need are normally present in any fertile soil. Any that are lacking will usually be supplied in amongst other substances through natural gardening techniques.

The only two micro-elements that plants do occasionally run short of are magnesium and boron. They usually only run short of them on very fast-draining soils. Natural gardening techniques usually overcome even that potential shortage.

Just as people have to eat the right foods if they are to remain healthy, so do plants. You can ensure that there is plenty of hydrogen, carbon and oxygen available to them by making sure that the structure of your soil is right. You can ensure that there is plenty of nitrogen, phosphorus and potassium available to them by feeding the soil correctly along organic gardening lines. The only place you might run into problems is in ensuring that there is sufficient calcium available to the plants.

The problem with calcium is not normally that the soil is short of it. Most soils contain plenty of it — although some vegetable crops like an extra helping. The problem is whether your soil is acid or alkaline. This is known as your pH factor — pH = potential of hydrogen.

Acid or Alkaline.

All soils are rated as acid, alkaline or neutral. It is important to know which you have got because some plants like acid soils, others like alkaline soils and *vice versa*. Apart from which you may want to change your soil from one to the other, or from either to neutral. In order to do that you need to know how acid or alkaline your soil is to start with.

The acidity or alkalinity of your soil is measured in terms of its hydrogen ion content. A soil with an excess of hydrolyx (OH–) is alkaline. When there are equal quantities of hydrogen ions and hydrolyx ions in the soil they combine to form water. The degree of acidity or alkalinity in a soil is measured by the concentration of hydrogen ions in it, and is expressed as a pH figure.

The pH scale runs from 0 to 14 where 0 is roughly as acid as hydrochloric acid and 14 is approximately as caustic as caustic soda. These extreme figures are only likely to be found under the most extreme conditions — such as in volcanic lava flows. The normal gardening range runs from about 4.5 to not much over 8.5. pH 7 is regarded as dead-centre neutral soil, but for most gardening purposes a pH figure of between 6.5 and 7.5 is regarded as neutral. The important thing to remember about the pH scale is that the figures on it bear a logarithmic relationship to each other, very much as do the *f* numbers on camera. The distance on the scale between pH 6.5 and pH 5.5 is twice that between 7.5 and 6.5 — and so on.

All this may sound very academic, but it is not. Your soil pH determines very largely what plants you can and cannot grow. The great majority of plants are happiest around a neutral pH figure or slightly on the acid side of neutral — between pH 6.5 and pH 7. Lilacs, by contrast, do best at pH 8, most heathers like a pH of about 5.5, while rhododendrons are best between pH 5.5 and 4.5. Hydrangeas turn blue at pH 5. Beyond the normal extremes of pH 8 and pH 4.5 only highly specialized plants will grow. Even surprisingly few rhododendrons will flourish if the pH is much more acid than 4.5, and they are a notoriously acid-loving group of plants.

In the United Kingdom most of those gardeners whose prime interest in gardening is growing decorative plants would, given the option between an acid and alkaline soil, choose the acid soil. In Britain's relatively mild, maritime climate they can grow rhododendrons (over 500 species and possibly as many as 5,000 hybrids), azaleas, camellias (of which again there are probably well in excess of 5,000 named varieties available), heathers, and a vast range of related *Ericaceae* and *Epadicraceae*, as well as most of the magnolias and their relatives. On a chalk soil the range of plants seems to most gardeners to be more limited: actually it is not – but denied the spectacular glory of rhododendrons, camellias and most magnolias, it possibly seems that way. More practical-minded gardeners, aware that we live in a world running out of resources, money and food, would opt for a neutral soil, which is best for the great majority of food crops.

In general, however, extreme soil types are to be avoided, and acid soils in particular present very real problems to anyone concerned with growing healthy plants in a healthy soil. Any soil that contains substances poisonous to plants cannot be regarded as healthy. Acid soils are particularly inclined to contain two particular poisons – carbon dioxide, due to the poor aeration which characterizes so many acid soils – and two metals – aluminium and manganese, both of which are typically present in relatively large quantities in acid soils. In addition acid soils are often short of calcium.

The problems presented by alkaline soils are generally less severe – though if you want to grow acid-loving plants on them you do have considerable problems.

While it may be of passing intellectual interest to know that your soil can be acid, alkaline or neutral, it is of very real practical value to know which in fact it is. There are several ways you can find out. If you are a born natural observer, look at the vegetation, both wild and cultivated: that will tell you quite a lot. Start by looking at the cultivated plants in your garden or other gardens in your street. If everyone in sight is growing rhododendrons and camellias, you live on an acid soil. If there is not a rhododendron in sight for miles around the soil is alkaline, and if lilacs abound on all sides, it is very alkaline. If your hydrangeas are all pink, your soil is alkaline and if they are blue it is acid: they blue at pH 5. One or two hydrangeas remain pink even on acid soils — so it is only if every hydrangea in your county is pink you can be sure you are on an alkaline soil .

Wild plants can tell you quite a lot too. Bracken or brake *Pteris aquilinium* only grows on very acid soils. Groundsel only grows on very alkaline soils. But do not be too worried if you have groundsel in front of your home and bracken behind it: soils can vary that much in that short a distance. This is when you want to test your soil, you need to take samples from several parts of the garden.

Soil testing is undoubtedly the most accurate way of determining the pH of your soil. There are two ways you can do this. Either delegate it, or do it yourself. If you choose to delegate, send samples for analysis to, in the United Kingdom your local county horticultural officer, in the United States of America to your State Agricultural Experimental Station. If you do this state quite clearly whether you want a pH analysis or a full analysis. If you ask for a full analysis you will get one — but you may not know what all the answers mean. They will tell you, if you want, your soil type, particle size, and humus content; they will tell you which of the minerals essential to plant growth are present, and in what quantities, and which are absent, as well as any toxic substances in your soil. All of which could be more than you wanted to know. If you are a technically-minded person it is the ideal way of doing things. Otherwise test the soil yourself solely to determine its pH value. Kits can be bought from many chemists and from most garden centres. They come complete with full instructions on how to use them and on what the results tell you. But all they will tell you is the pH of your soil.

An ideal soil in which to grow healthy plants is slightly on the acid side of neutral, between pH 6.5 and pH 7. Corrective measures can be taken to deal with both extremes of acidity and alkalinity, and these will be dealt with in the next chapter.

3 / Improving Your Soil

Whatever sort of soil you live on, you will probably wish you lived on some other sort of soil. If you live on a heavy-to-work, slow-draining clay soil, you will probably wish you lived on a sand soil. If you live on a nutrient-impoverished fast-draining sand soil, you will probably wish you lived on good loam. If you live on good loam count yourself lucky and keep working on that soil, because even good loams deteriorate if mishandled. If your soil is alkaline you will probably wish you lived on an acid soil, and if it is acid you will probably wish at least part of it was neutral so your vegetables would do better. Take heart, whatever sort of soil you live on, you can improve it beyond recognition. If you follow the advice given in this book you could literally turn a slag heap of 0.1ha/¼ acre into a garden vibrant with flowers, fruit and vegetables in not so very many years.

It may seem a very facile thing to say, but you can improve any basic soil type, and most extreme soil types too, simply by adding humus. There is just one rider: provided your drainage is right. So, if you are setting about a programme of soil improvement – and good soil is the key to success in natural gardening – the first thing to look at is drainage. After that look at the role of humus in improving your soil, and then look at changing your soil pH.

Drainage.
There are three reasons why your soil might be badly drained. The most likely is quite simply that the mineral particles of which it is largely composed could be so fine that there are no pores be-

tween them large enough to allow water to drain through freely.

The second most likely reason is that there is some sort of obstruction to drainage not in the soil itself but in the subsoil, possibly quite deep down 1m+/4ft, such as a thick layer of impervious clay or hardpan.

The third reason is quite simply that your garden is below the level of the water-table for your area. In which case the normal level of water in the soil is above the depth to which the roots usually penetrate.

You must first find out which of these is your drainage problem, if indeed you have a drainage problem: many people do not. Analysis of your soil particle size should already have told you whether you have problems with the drainage in your top-soil. If you have that is fairly easily dealt with. Copious applications of humus, combined on some soils with coarse sand or grit will usually solve that.

Having established whether your top-soil is draining sufficiently freely, you then need to establish whether the water that drains through can get away through the layers below. There is only one way to find out. Dig a hole, and dig it deep. For most normal gardening activities a hole 1m+/4ft deep and 1m/3ft across should be sufficient, which can be hard work. If you hit bedrock before you get that deep, you have got a highly specialized problem: consult your county horticultural officer in the United Kingdom or, in the United States of America your State Agricultural Experimental Station. Assuming you have not hit bedrock and have managed to dig your 1m+/4ft hole all you do is sit back and see whether or not it fills with water. Do not dig the hole during heavy rains: apart from making it much more difficult to dig, it will fill up with water while you dig it. The picture you get will be untypical. So try to choose a season to dig when heavy rains are not imminent.

Having dug your hole what you then do is watch to see the amount of water that runs off into it from surrounding soil, and how fast any water that collects in it after heavy rains takes to drain away.

There are two sets of circumstances which indicate a need for deep soil drainage action on your part. The first is if the hole starts filling with water from the surrounding soil even though additional rain has not fallen – or if the hole starts filling while you are still digging it. Both show that your water table is very high. Under such conditions the hole, once dug, is likely to remain substantially filled with water until you fill it again with soil. The second is, if the hole remains relatively dry except after heavy rains: if after heavy rains the water takes more than four to five days to drain completely that again shows that you have bad drainage, but for a different reason. Your water table may be 10m/30ft below the bottom of your hole, but something is preventing the water draining through into it.

In both cases you need to lay land drains to solve the problem effectively, but what you do with the water that comes out of those land drains will differ. Let us look at the land drains first.

Land drains are quite simply unglazed (therefore porous) clay pipes. Each pipe is cleanly cut at one end, but has a neck or shoulder at the other. The pipes are always laid so that the shoulder is higher on the slope than the clean-cut end. The two slip into each other. As they lie fitted into each other in this way on a downhill gradient water enters the drainage pipes primarily through the junction between one pipe and the next at the shoulder point. Further water enters the pipes simply because they are porous, though that in itself cannot normally be relied upon as adequate to cope with the drainage demands that might arise in heavy rainfall periods. The pipes themselves should be surrounded by several inches of coarse stones or pebbles, which themselves increase drainage and help to focus the water into the land drains.

To lay the drains properly the first thing you need to do is study the lie of your land. If there is even the slightest slope on it, mark the lowest point, and drain all your surplus water towards that. If your land is dead level, choose your own terminal drainage point. In a small garden, a quarter acre or so, one terminal point will be sufficient. In larger gardens, 0.4ha/1 acre or more, you may need several terminal points. Lay these as individual systems each like the one outlined below.

Start by sticking a flag in the ground where you want your drains to terminate. For ease of explanation but also for ease of laying, it helps if this point can be in or close to a corner of your plot. Then draw a line diagonally across your plot from the opposite corner to the terminal point. The line will become, as it were, the spine of your drainage system. You will then need to mark similarly the secondary drains leading into the spine drain.

These should be equidistant, but staggered from both sides so that they enter the spine drain from each side alternately. The spacing of the drains will depend upon just how severe a drainage problem you have. A reasonable average spacing would be 5m/15ft between drains on each side of the spine drain. Where large areas with very severe drainage problems are concerned a spacing of 3m/10ft is preferable. Any secondary drains more than 6m/20ft long should have tertiary drains running into them.

The shallowest any land drain should be laid in a garden is 30cm/12in. Shallower than that and they will be damaged by cultivation activities and by the action of frost – rarely in the United Kingdom but quite frequently in hard winter zones in the United States. That is 30cm/12in to the top of the drain. If you are using 15cm/6in drains, and you are bedding them in gravel, dig the trench 45cm/18in deep to start with.

Then determine the gradient of the fall you want. Go for the sharpest fall your soil conditions and strength will run to. The minimum workable drop is 2.5cm/1in in 2m/6ft. Less than that and the drains will silt up so fast you will be relaying them every year or two. A fall of 2.5cm/1in in 1m/3ft is far better to aim for. All drains feed into the spine drain which in turn empties into a sump.

To lay land drains start by digging your sump at the point marked by your flag. The shallowest you can dig it is so that it penetrates the impermeable layer of soil which is causing the bad drainage. The deeper you dig it the longer it will last. However carefully you lay the drains, however carefully you surround them with gravel, soil particles will get washed into them, and from them into the sump. In time they will slow down the rate at which the sump drains. Should they impede drainage in the sump completely, you would be back to square one. A minimum workable size for a sump is 1m/3ft across. Make it larger if you can, if only because it is easier to work. The easy thing to do with your sump is just to fill it in with broken bricks, large chunks of rock or whatever coarse drainage materials are to hand. The right way to do it is to dig the sides vertically downwards and line them with bricks. Use a drywalling technique (no mortar) below the impermeable soil layer (this will allow water to seep out of the sides of the sump as well as through its base), and mortared brickwork above the impermeable layer – not forgetting of course to set the emptying drain into the brickwork. The usual thing to do having got this far is to fill the whole thing with broken bricks and other coarse drainage materials, level it off, and forget about it. If you are ecologically minded you can line the bottom of your brickwork with heavy-duty plastic sheeting, providing yourself with an overgrown water butt. Leave a few courses of permeable brickwork above that, before your mortared brickwork collar. Build an ornamental well-head and use the water in the bottom of your sump for irrigation in summer .

Dig your trenches four square and straight back up the garden from your sump. Check that your fall is right as you dig, and again when you have finished digging and before you lay the land drains. It pays to do the job properly. If you do, your land drains should last you twenty years or more, short of a seismological catastrophe.

If, however, you live where a very high water table is your problem and there is no way you can dig down deep enough to create a drainage sump, the only option left to you is to use the water as an ornamental feature in your garden. You still drain it off the bulk of the land laying a herringbone pattern of land drains. The only difference is that instead of the water then being able to seep away into deeper ground, you will have it all collected together in one corner of your garden. Faced with this situation you may prefer to move your water nearer centre. Make the most of the water you collect in this way. Use it as a garden pool.

You might well think that in a garden with this particular problem there is no need to line the sump, since the whole land area is waterlogged anyway. In fact it does need lining, because unless you line it the water you have so carefully collected in one place by means of your land drains will immediately flow back into the land you have just drained. The simplest way of lining the pool is to use heavy-duty plastic sheeting. It does pay, however, to secure the point at which the water enters the pool from the land drains with brickwork. The purpose of this is to keep the drain as stable as possible. If it slips out of position the drains will simply feed their water back into the drained area.

To make the system work really well you need more than one pool. Firstly you need a very tiny pool, which is no more than a settlement tank (which collects any silt flowing down the land drains) but which also acts as an air-break on the land drains. It needs either to drain into a larger pool at a lower level or have a system by which water is pumped from this small tank into the larger pool. If the land drains feed the pool direct, once the water rises above the level of the terminal land drain it will simply draw water back up it. Ideally the big pool should overflow into a marginal area.

In countries, and areas generally, where high water table problems are widespread it is often possible to pump your water up and out of your pond into a public drainage channel. Where this is not possible you need to disperse the water as rapidly as possible. The only way you can do this is to use plants. But use those that do it best.

All plants pump water up through their roots, and use this water in the process of photosynthesis. A by-product of photosynthesis is that plants give off water in the form of vapour at a surprisingly high rate. It is known as transpiration. A silver birch *Betula papifera* not so very big – 5m/15ft – with upwards of 5,000,000 leaves will transpire 68–90 litres/15–20 Imperial gallons in a day under grey skies – even in rain. In full sun in hot weather it will transpire 900 litres/40 gallons or more in a day. A small clump of these trees, five or seven, planted closely could pump two hundred gallons of water a day. Bog plants like the giant *Gunnera manicata* have a similarly surprising capacity for transpiring water. Trees that normally grow with their feet in the water are even more efficient at this. The problem is that the great majority are deciduous, which means that they are pumping no water at all out of your land or sump in winter when your water level will be at its highest. You need evergreens. While there are plenty of suitable plants readily available to anyone living in the subtropical zones of the United States of America, there are relatively few evergreens that will grow in bog conditions in cold winter areas and most of those that will are dwarf plants. By far the best wintergreen water pumping trees are the piceas, and only one of these is really happy with its feet in the water.

Picea sitchensis. If a tightly packed clump of these is densely under-planted with the most vigorous of the hardy bamboos, especially those of the *Phyllostachus* group, this should provide sufficient pumping power to attain a reasonable degree of control of the water level even in winter. Assuming that you either have no need to lay land drains or that you have already done so, the next aspect of improving your soil that needs to be looked at is concerned with improving the drainage of the topsoil itself — the area where the greatest root activity takes place, and this in itself is very largely a matter of incorporating humus.

The Function of Humus.

Quite what you expect humus to do to your topsoil will depend largely on how you are using the word humus. In the sense in which it is normally used, especially by organic gardening enthusiasts — as decayed or decaying vegetable matter such as compost, farmyard manure, peat and so on — it will do one thing to the soil. In the stricter sense of microscopic colloidal particles it will do something else.

There is a widespread belief that humus in its looser sense will improve any soil. Probably this is true. What these bulky, organic substances do is to open up the soil structure, to increase the airspaces between the mineral and other particles, thereby improving both drainage and aeration. At the same time, they soften the surface of the soil increasing the proportion of any precipitation which is actually absorbed. Humus also retains the water at a level in the soil where it is readily accessible to plants for longer than would be the case with soils where bulky organic matter is absent. However, on certain soils, especially peat soils, which are already too rich in organic matter, they will do little good and could actually make the drainage problem worse.

The role of humus in the strict sense of black and brown colloidal particles of organic matter is less well understood, although it is currently the subject of a considerable amount of research. It has definitely been established that humus in this sense is beneficial in clay soils. The humus particles combine with the colloidal clay particles and cause the clay crumbs to have larger pores through their bodies. This means not only that the clay then drains better but also that it is easier to work. Water held in suspension in the pores of clay improved by the addition of colloidal humus particles is more readily available to the plants, and that in turn makes the nutrients, in which clay is very rich, more readily accessible to the plants too. There is no doubt whatsoever that humus, both in its looser and in its stricter sense, has a beneficial effect on clay soils.

The role of humus in the strict sense upon sand soils is less well understood. Until relatively recently sand soils have been thought to be fast draining and therefore to present few problems to gardeners. It is only relatively recently that it has been realized that many sand soils are not in fact fast draining, but often so poorly drained as to produce almost anaerobic conditions. It is this realization that has encouraged research into the role of humus in relation to sand soils. While the reasons are not yet fully understood there is no doubt at all that many sand soils can only be kept productive when they are liberally supplied with humus in its looser sense. If this is the case it would seem that it is not the black and brown colloidal humus particles which are producing the beneficial results, but rather the slow-decaying fibres so often found in garden compost and in farm and stable manure. What these do is to space the sand particles out further than they would otherwise be, thereby creating sufficiently large pores between the particles for effective drainage and aeration to occur. If these preliminary findings are correct then the types of organic matter that should be used on sand soils are those which are most bulky and most fibrous – compost, farmyard or horse manure containing an abundance of straw, and the wastes from natural fibre factories and processing plants. Manures like sewage sludge, poultry manure and guano should be carefully avoided.

Improving Specific Soil Types.

Although it is a fairly acceptable generalization to say that bulky organic sources of humus will improve most soils, different soil types do require slightly different treatments.

Sand Soils. Although sand soils are generally easily to recognize, they vary enormously among themselves and for this reason present some problems when you want to set about improving them. The first thing you need to know is just what sort of sand soil you live on. The extremes vary between sand soils with particle sizes as large as 1mm diameter, which will be extremely fast draining, and sand soils with particle sizes as small as 0.05mm, which will be very poorly drained indeed. The only way you can find out which you have is to filter the particles through laboratory filters as recommended in Chapter One. You will probably find you have a mixture of particle sizes. Those of which you have most by bulk are the determining ones.

If your soil particles are large, and you have a fast-draining sand soil, add all the bulky humus you can, and dig it thoroughly into the topsoil. Then, on those areas set down to permanent plantings, mulch annually and mulch heavily, 8–10cm/3–4in of mixed leaf-mould and farmyard manure if you can get it – compost if you cannot. Dig similar amounts into areas where you can dig.

If you find your sand soil has a very small particle size the most effective thing you can do is to garden on top of the soil rather than in it. Bulky organic materials dug into the soil will do little good. The same materials added to the surface of the soil will do an enormous amount of good. Over the years you will find that you have not only built up a good layer of workable soil above the level at which you started, but that micro-organisms and earthworms will have carried it down to deeper levels of the soil, improving that too. However, they will have done this relatively slowly and relatively selectively.

On any sand soil always use the bulkiest organic manures you can obtain, especially those which contain a high proportion of vegetable fibre. Avoid any sludgy, semi-liquid manures.

Clay soils.   Organic manures are the prime soil improver here too, but they are not generally enough on their own. Since the drainage problems of clay soils are caused by their minute mineral particles, one of the quickest ways of improving them is to add sharp sand as well as bulky manures. The sand should be really sharp, with a particle size of anything from 0.05mm to 2mm. If you can obtain it, an ideal course of action would be to add one part sand to four parts organic manure by bulk very year until you are satisfied that you have converted your clay soil to a good loam: then keep on with the treatment for a further five years, otherwise the soil will start to go back on you. Even when you have done that, it will only remain in good heart so long as you continue to maintain it along similar lines.

The old ideas of double trenching and bastard trenching as a way of dealing with clay are now known to do little good. Humus is useless buried a couple of spits down in the soil. The only soil organisms that can make use of it live near the surface, in the top

30cm/12in, so putting the manure further down is really wasting it. You might as well save the manure and save the energy for something more rewarding.

If you are breaking virgin soil, dig it over as best you can, and then cover it with a 10-15cm/4-6in layer of mixed manure and sharp sand. Leave it over winter then, once the soil warms up in spring and dries out sufficiently to be workable, lightly fork it into the surface. The following year dig it in a little deeper, the year after a little deeper. If you try to bring up an extra 5cm/2in of clay each time you go through this routine, you will find you will have a good workable depth of highly productive soil 30-46cm/12-18in deep in as little as five or eight years.

As with sandy soils, it is the organic substances that contain plenty of fibre that will produce the most rapid results on clay soil. Once you have the clay soil into a healthy state the type of manure you use becomes less critical.

Loam Soils. So far as structure goes there is a very little need to take any action to improve these, since their structure is already well-nigh perfect. The reason for using organic manures on them is mainly to replace the goodness taken out by crops and so on. This being the case, a light dressing of sharp sand once a year, preferably in late summer/early winter, will ensure that the soil does not deteriorate, since the addition of only organic manures, especially sludgy ones, could in time tend to clog some of the free pores in the soil.

Stony Soils. As with sandy soils, but for different reasons, often the easiest option here is to garden above your soil rather than in it. If the soil is extremely stony, virtually the only substance into which any plants you attempt to grow can put their roots are the organic materials you bring onto the site. The more bulky manure or compost you add the better. If your soil is not extremely stony, but only moderately stony, you will be tempted to take out the stones. After all, where there is a stone there could be a root, and roots are more use to plants than stones. There is a golden rule here. If you take a stone out, put a handful of coarse sand back. If you do not the soil will pan on you.

Peat Soils. These present a peculiar dilemma to the organic gardener, since they are already composed almost entirely of organic matter. The problem here is not that they lack humus but that they lack nutrients and drainage. The first thing to tackle is the drainage, preferably with land drains. The next thing is to add organic manures or compost in equal parts by bulk with sharp sand — as for clay soils. Again, as for clay soils, dig these two a little deeper each year. The sand is probably more important here than the organic manure, but so long as you use a really sharp sand the type of liquid sludge manures that are unsuitable for most other types of soil will be ideal for peat soils.

Gumbo or Adobe Soils.   This is one of those extreme soil types that are actually extremely rich in plant foods and yet tend to look about as barren as can be. The cause of this barren look is lack of soil-moisture content. The recipe, as for muck soils, is to dig in all the bulky organic material you can. Its function here is not to feed the soil, not even to open its crumb structure, but quite simply to act as a sponge to hold water. Once the water is there the natural fertility of soils of this type will become apparent very quickly.

A further problem with most soils, but it reaches extreme proportions in peat and gumbo soils, is that they may be too acid (peat soils) or too alkaline (gumbo soils) for the plants to be able to take up the nutrients in them. Even with less extreme types of soil it is pretty usual to have to take steps to adjust the soil pH, either to suit the needs of the plants you want to grow, or in order to grow specialist plants or crops.

Adjusting Your pH.
As explained earlier, most plants grow best in a soil that is just on your soil will change its pH, fractionally each time, but just be lucky enough to have a soil that is already between these tolerances, but even if you have, read on, because the pH value of your soil will change over the years. Soot, exhaust fumes from internal combustion engines and some type of industrial pollution will gradually make it more acid: other types of industrial pollution will make it more alkaline. If you use a lot of peat you will tend to make it more acid: if you use a lot of nitrogen-rich compost you may make it more alkaline. The very plants you grow on your soil will change its pH, fractionally each time, but

cumulatively the change could be significant. For this reason you should monitor your soil pH, taking readings not less than once in every two years.

To make an acid soil neutral you add lime. The problem here is that the word lime has been so much used and misused over the years that a considerable confusion has arisen as to just what is meant by lime. There are in fact three sorts of lime. (1) Quicklime = burnt lime = calcium oxide = CaO. (2) Slaked lime = hydrated lime = calcium hydroxide = Ca (OH). (3) Ground limestone = ground chalk = carbonate of lime = $CaCo_3$. Number One – quicklime – should be avoided. It is not particularly effective at changing acidity to alkalinity, and its effect on the soil is very short-lived. Apart from that it is extremely unpleasant stuff to handle: it will literally burn your hands if you touch it; it also burns up many soil organisms, the vast majority of them beneficial. Beyond that it can burn the roots of newly set out transplants. Number 2 – slaked lime – is somewhat more desirable. It does not burn your hands, your soil organisms or your plant roots. Its main advantage is that it is relatively readily obtainable: its main disadvantage is that you need enormous quantities of it to have any real effect on your soil pH. Number 3 – ground limestone or chalk – is much to be preferred. You need relatively small applications of it, and these last quite a long time in the ground. A good liming with ground limestone should be effective for between four and five years on a good loam soil. The finest of several types of ground limestone available is ground Dolomitic Limestone, since it contains magnesium which is deficient in many soils.

When liming soils to raise the pH figure towards neutral considerable care should be taken over the rate of application, since over-liming can do as much or more damage than not liming at all. The first point is that you should never try to alter the pH figure by more than one digit on the scale (i.e. from pH 4.5 to pH 5.5) in any season. The soil simply cannot cope with greater doses than that. The lime not only alters the pH, it also alters the structure of the soil, usually tending to make it more open and free-draining, but it also affects the micro-organisms. As you change your soil pH you change a large proportion of your soil population. Like plants, most of them can only live between certain pH tolerances. Change your pH radically and you could wipe out a very large proportion of the soil population that is so essential to the healthy growth of your plants. By changing the soil pH gradually those that cannot survive at the altered level will migrate. While those that prefer the new level will increase in numbers. If you are adding bulky organic matter to the soil at the same time as liming it, you will be introducing new soil organisms which can optimize the new soil pH level. But the change must be a gradual one.

Manufacturers, or rather packagers of lime are very much inclined to tell you to apply the lime at x grammes or x lbs per m² or sq yd. Life is not that simple. Different types of soil respond to lime at different rates. For example, it takes only 1.8kg/4lbs of lime to raise a light, sandy soil from pH 4.5 to pH 5, but it takes 4.5kg/10lbs to raise a heavy clay soil by the same amount. When liming consult the table on p.50. Just as acid soils can be made into neutral soils by the application of lime, so too are there substances which will turn alkaline soils into neutral or, if you require it, acid soils. In the United States of America the two materials most widely recommended for making an alkaline soil neutral or acid are powdered sulphur and aluminium sulphate. The usual recommendation is that of the two powdered sulphur is to be preferred, if only because you need only one-sixth as much (by bulk) to achieve the same lowering of the pH figure. Furthermore it is cheaper than aluminium sulphate.

On no account should aluminium sulphate be used for neutralizing an alkaline soil. It leaves deposits of aluminium in the soil which are readily absorbed by plants. Aluminium is poisonous to plants: it is also poisonous to people, and obviously if used on a vegetable patch could cause illness quite quickly. Besides, once in the soil, it is very slow to degenerate or get leached out.

Powdered sulphur is less obnoxious, provided it is only used where ornamental plants are being grown. It, too, is toxic and best not used in the garden at all.

Having thus effectively ruled out your two quickest means of neutralizing an alkaline soil, two options remain open to you. Both are effective, but both take slightly longer to achieve their results. The first is the liberal use of a moss peat with a high acid reaction. Forked into the top 20cm/8in of the soil it will quite quickly make the soil less alkaline. If a programme of digging in moss peat and mulching with moss peat is kept up over a number of years the change in the pH figure can be dramatic. The process can be

LIMING CHART

This shows the amount of hydrated lime required to raise the pH value to 6.5 on different types of soil. The rates are for application over areas of 90m²/100ft²

pH	Soil Acidity	Light Sandy Soil	Sandy Loam or Silt Soils	Medium Soils Loam	Clay Soils	Heavy Clay
6	Moderate	0.91kg/2lbs	1.36kg/3lbs	1.82kg/4lbs	2.27kg/5lbs	2.72kg/6lbs
5.5	Strong	1.36kg/3lbs	1.82kg/4lbs	2.36kg/5¾lbs	3.18kg/7lbs	3.27kg/7¾lbs
5.0	Very strong	1.42kg/3¾lbs	2.36kg/5¾lbs	3.21kg/7¼lbs	3.64kg/8lbs	4.12kg/9¼lbs
4.5	Extreme	1.82kg/4lbs	2.78kg/6½lbs	3.64kg/8lbs	3.73kg/8¾lbs	4.54kg/10lbs

speeded up by ensuring that you use only bulky organic manures of a high acid reaction, and avoiding those with an alkaline reaction.

So far we have looked at bulky organic materials only in terms of the effect they can have on improving the structure of the soil. Now it is time to look at their relative food value, because plants need more than just a good soil structure to be healthy: they need the right nutrients too. That is what the next chapter is about.

4 / Feeding Your Plants

In Chapter Two we took a quick glance at what plants need from the soil. In this chapter we take a more practical look at how you can supply your plants with the foods they need.

The first requirements of any plant are air and water freely available to its roots: if they do not have these two essential items you might as well forget about feeding them. They will die anyway. By improving your soil along the lines suggested in the previous chapter you can ensure that your plants' air and water needs are adequately met.

Their next requirement is minerals, which are taken up by the roots in the form of a week solution of mineral salts. Obviously plants can only take up these salts if they are available in the soil, and if there is sufficient water held in tension in the soil particles for them to be able to absorb them.

The most important of the foods needed by plants are calcium, nitrogen, phosphorus and potassium. In general there is plenty of calcium available to plants in any healthy, fertile soil. It is sometimes deficient in extremely acid soils, but this deficiency can readily be corrected by liming, or, if you want to use only organic substances, by the use of broken egg-shells, powdered bone, bonemeal and other feeds made from calcium-rich sources.

It is the other three, nitrogen, phosphorus and potassium that plants draw on very heavily and which need to be constantly replenished in order to keep a good soil healthy. If you buy a 'complete' fertilizer, you will find it is these three that it contains. It does not contain any calcium. Manufacturers of fertilizers are required by law, both in the United States of America and the United

Kingdom to state the relative quantities of each of the three plant foods on the package. The three are represented by the short-form of their chemical symbol, nitrogen = N, phosphorus = P and potassium = K. On artificial fertilizer packages the three are always stated in the same order. Thus a 10/10/10 artificial fertilizer is 10 parts N = nitrogen, 10 part P = phosphorus and 10 parts K = potassium. A 6/12/18 fertilizer is 6 parts nitrogen, 12 parts phosphorus and 18 parts potassium. This is very nice and neat and tidy, because if you buy yourself a packet of artificial fertilizer you know exactly what proportions of which plant food you are applying, and at what rate you apply it. In America many manufacturers have started adding trace elements, mainly boron and magnesium to 'complete' artificial fertilizers. This is on the 'play safe' principle. There is no harm in adding these elements since the plants will not use them unless they need them. You just waste more of your money. However, the fact that manufacturers of 'complete' fertilizers are adding these elements is a tacit ad-mission of the incompleteness of complete artificial fertilizers.

If you are reading this book you probably do not need con-vincing that artificial fertilizers are a bad thing. You may not be aware of why they are a bad thing. The reason why they should be avoided in the garden is that, although they may feed the plants adequately – though recently some doubt has been cast as to whether they do in fact do that – they do nothing whatsoever for the soil. They certainly do nothing at all to improve its texture, its crumb structure or any other aspect of its structural health. In fact they do rather the opposite. They tend in time to degrade the soil. In agriculture, where heavy reliance has been placed on arti-ficial fertilizers over very long periods, the soil has become so degraded that the structure of the soil has collapsed. We have already seen how important the structure of the soil is to healthy plant growth. In extreme cases the over-use of artificial fertilizers has caused the soil structure to collapse to such an extent that even in the warm, wet climate of England the soil has just blown away on the wind. The manufacturers of artificial fertilizers have now come up with a chemical which 'glues' the soil particles back together again so that farmers can go on using still more artificial fertilizers. This is not the answer. What the soil needs is a proper structure, and a proper structure is one which contains a high pro-portion of organic matter.

There are two other interrelated reasons why it is sensible to avoid the use of artificial fertilizers in the home garden. The first is cost, the second is efficiency. The price of the raw materials of which artificial fertilizers are made is about to escalate in a way you have never seen prices escalate before. The cost of producing nitrogen has risen by over 300% in the past seven years. The cost of potassium has risen by nearly 400% in the last two years, and the cost of phosphorus, the rarest of the three, by a staggering 700% in under a year. While costs rise, effectiveness diminishes. Take virgin land and apply a 'complete' artificial fertilizer to it, and on average you can double the crop yield. In the second year the yield will be down a little, and in the third year it will be down even further. After ten to fifteen years yields are virtually the same as they were before you applied artificial fertilizer, unless you increase the rate of application of the artificial fertilizer – which is what usually happens. It can take as much as thirty times the original application of artificial fertilizer to raise the yield from land that has been fed artificial fertilizer for periods of longer than twenty years by 1% as it did in the first year of application to raise it by 100%. In terms of cost-effectiveness artificial fertilizers are useless in the long term. The only people to benefit from their use are the shareholders. Certainly the soil does not benefit, nor do the plants, nor do the people who eat the plants.

Finally, and perhaps most detrimental of all, is the simple fact that artificial fertilizers do nothing to encourage healthy soil populations. Over a period of years their build-up in the soil tends rather to poison and kill the soil population: if it has not already died because the crumb structure of the soil has collapsed.

There is only one proper way to feed soil, and that is with bulky, organic manures. That, after all, is how plants fed themselves before artificial manures were invented. And how they will go on feeding themselves long after artificial fertilizer manufacturers have gone out of business. Bulky organic manures not only supply plants with the food they need in a form readily acceptable to the plants, they also improve the structure of the soil and encourage thriving soil populations. Most bulky organic manures are a mixture of animal excreta and straw or some similar bedding material. The problem is that the more urbanized and sub-urbanized we become the further afield the sources of the organic manures become. Nonetheless, animals there are, and if animals eat they must excrete. And animals do eat. What is more they often eat in enclosed conditions of forced-rearing where their manure is readily collectable. The tragedy is that, in the United Kingdom for example, the pig farmers produce some 5,000,000 tons of pig manure a year, and they do not know what to do with it. It just lies in their backyards, smelling rather strongly.

NUTRIENT RELATIVITIES TABLE

The approximate NPK content of some commonly available organic manures

MATERIAL	%N	%P	%K
Blood and Bone	6.5	7.0	—
Bone Meal	3.0	15.0	—
Good Garden Compost	1.5	2.0	0.7
Cow Manure	0.6	0.4	0.3
Dried Blood	13.0	2.0	1.0
Farmyard Manure	0.6	0.4	0.5
Fish Meal	10.0	4.0	—
Hoof and Horn	12.0	2.0	—
Horse Manure	0.7	0.5	0.6
Pig Manure	0.5	0.3	0.4
Poultry Manure	1.6	1.8	7.0
Sewage Sludge	0.5	0.5	0.2
Town Waste	1.2	0.5	0.3
Sedge Peat	1.0	1.5	0.6
Moss Peat	0.5	1.0	0.3
Spent Hops	0.4	1.2	2.0
Seaweed	0.3	1.3	2.3

NOTE: these quantities are only approximate, as they must be. A horse, for example, is not a carefully contrived machine for making manure, and the relative NPK content of horse manure will depend to some extent on the health of the horse and what it had for breakfast. Similarly the NPK content of your compost bin will vary: the %N will increase if you use a lot of eggshells, for example.

The other problem, if problem it is (and it may be to the tidy-minded) is that while you can buy artificial fertilizers knowing that they contain exactly 10 parts N, 10 parts P and 10 parts K, animals have not yet been taught to excrete the waste-products of their digestive tracts in neatly balanced bundles. You cannot, in all reasonableness, stand behind a horse with a shovel and expect it to produce a neat bundle of 8/5/8 for you: nor can you expect a cow to produce 6/12/18 for you. However, for the great majority of bulky organic manures the approximate NPK content is known. These are listed on p.55. The figures are only approximate: they alter with the age of the manure, with what the animal ate and for many other reasons. At best, figures like these can only give approximate guidance as to which manures are rich in which elements.

However, if you have difficulty obtaining these bulky manures, there is another option open to you. Your garden compost. A quick look at the chart shows that good garden compost is one of the best-balanced of all bulky organic manures. Even if you can readily obtain other organic manures, you will also need garden compost. Reliance on any one of the other manures could lead to nutrient imbalance. The use of garden compost will level-off any possibility of this. What is more, you should be able to supply all your own organic manure needs from your own compost heap from materials already on your own premises. In this respect you can be completely self-sufficient.

The Compost Bin.

If you ever heard of compost heaps, forget them. They were simply an untidy mound of garden waste, where people used to dump garden debris. Over the years it would sprawl further and further across the garden, becoming ever untidier and untidier.

A compost bin is something quite different. It is a carefully designed, properly constructed bin in which normal garden and organic household waste can be converted into a rich, brown, spongy substance, with a texture very similar to high-grade sphagnum moss peat, which not only looks good and smells good, but also does your garden good. It is not only a first-rate source of humus, but also contains all the nutrients plants normally need. In short, it is the finest plant food you can get.

This is how you make it.

First of all you decide where you want your compost bin. To maximize your compost-making facility, do not just have one bin, have three: one complete, full and waiting to be used; one nearly full and nearing completion; and one just started. Some people go for four bins, which enables you to have at least two, sometimes three, filled and ready for use in one season.

The main criteria to bear in mind when siting your bins are these. Firstly, for efficient composting, the bins need to be in full sun, exposed to all the elements. Second, from your point of view, they need to be in a position that is easily accessible from the house, since a lot of household refuse can go onto them, and they need to be central to the garden, since you will be using the compost in all parts of the garden. All of which does not mean that your compost bins have to become the focal feature of your garden. You can screen them with fences, trellises covered in ornamental or fruiting vines, with hedges or decorative shrubs.

Second, buy or build yourself a bin or, preferably, a series of bins. There are many good models on the market. Shop around the garden centres, compare prices, sizes, materials, and match them against the criterion for good performance.

If you are going to build your own bins, the first thing to consider is shape. The most efficient bins are drum-shaped. It is difficult to construct a drum-shaped bin yourself. You can always use old oil or petrol drums, provided they are large enough, and provided you make so many holes all round them that there is about an equal area of perforations to solid matter. Simpler, and only slightly less efficient at composting, is a four-square bin. If you decide to settle for rectangular bins, make them as near square as possible. Make each bin a separate, free-standing entity. You need air circulating all round any compost bin, and this cannot happen if the bins have shared walls.

There are lots of materials from which you can build your bins. Your ultimate choice will probably be a compromise between what you want and what you can afford. You can build it out of wood — poles, split chestnut palings, planks — out of brick, stone, breeze blocks, steel girders and sheeting or concrete. Leave plenty of gaps between the solid matter: the bins need to breathe. Line the inside of the bins with chicken wire — preferably plastic coated or extruded — to prevent the contents of the bin from falling out through the spaces. Raise the bottom of the bin off the ground.

Use thick planks laid flat across breeze-blocks, then covered with chicken wire, or some similar technique, to make a gap between the bottom of the compost and the ground. Always keep this gap clear; use a rake to draw any waste matter that falls through back towards you and put it on top of the bin again.

If you are new to efficient compost-making techniques you are probably wondering why so much emphasis is being put on letting the bin breathe, and on ventilation at ground level. Think of it this way. Compost works like a bonfire, only instead of reducing garden refuse to ashes you reduce it to a peaty-humus rich material. Instead of flames doing the breaking down of the organic material, as in a bonfire, the compost heap is consumed by bacteria – billions of them. Like a flame, they need air to live. Like a bonfire too, bacteria consume most fastest when they have a good updraft. Like a bonfire too, compost gets hot: efficient, experienced compost makers can fill a bin and raise the temperature inside it to as high as $53.4^{\circ}C/160^{\circ}F$ in forty-eight hours – provided there is a good updraft. Research in Phoenix, Arizona, has shown that the bacteria inside a bin working at maximum efficiency can consume as much as $6.370m^3/20,000ft^3$ in 24 hours per $101kg/1$ ton. And if a ton of compost sounds a lot, it is not: that is what you can produce in a bin 120cm by 120cm/4ft by 4ft.

One last thought on design and construction. Do remember to make one side of the bin removable or detachable. It is no good building a marvellous compost bin if you cannot get the compost out afterwards.

Grist to the Mill.   If you have ever read anything on compost making by a compost fanatic of the type who swears his compost is good enough to eat (and may even eat it before your very eyes!) you will probably have gained the impression that one day, usually in autumn, they suddenly decide to make compost, and then they conjure, as by magic, from all parts of the garden, enough vegetable waste, lawn clippings and so on, to fill a bin, add a pinch of some magic ingredient, and the compost is ready a couple of weeks later. Forget it. It can be done, but it is not how gardens or compost heaps are normally run.

In practice a compost bin is a on-going concern. You do not make it suddenly one afternoon: you gradually fill the bin as and when the materials become available. Build the contents of the bin up like a multi-layered sandwich. When you have laid down about 15cm/6in vegetable matter, add a 5cm/2in layer of some non-green matter like garden soil, peat, leaf-mould, manure, then add more green waste. Keep doing this until the bin is full. Close it off with a final 5cm/2in layer of earth and move on to the next bin. If you use this 'cake' technique it does not matter too much how long it takes you to fill a bin. That will depend partly on what you put into it, partly on the size of your garden and a lot of other things. You may fill a bin a fortnight: it may take you a year. There is no golden rule as to how long it should take. The important thing is to fill one bin before starting to fill the next. However, if it takes you more than a year to fill the bin, you will find the materials at the bottom so much further composted than the materials at the top that you could run into problems when you want to use the compost in the garden.

As to what you do or do not put into your compost bin, that can, if you like, remain a secret between your bin and you. For guidance look at nature. After all, it is nature you are imitating. In the wild, in a forest, for example, humus, which is what you are making, occurs naturally as the results of leaf-fall, the decomposition of fallen trees and boughs, the withering of the leaves of undergrowth plants, of the droppings of the birds and animals that inhabit the forest and, in the end, of the decomposition of the animals themselves. Translated into garden terms this means that you can put any garden refuse into the bin; lawn clippings, green weeds, dry weeds, dead heads, uprooted haulms, yellowing leaves from ripening vegetables and so on. The nutrient value of your compost will be even higher if you supplement it with vegetable waste from the kitchen, potato peelings, pea and bean pods, yellowed cabbage leaves, even things like the contents of a half can of baked beans you opened and forgot to go back to finish. There is a lot of other rubbish produced in most households that will compost well. Old newspapers, (which compost best if shredded), old cardboard boxes torn into strips, the emptyings from the vacuum cleaner, scrapings from bird cages and the cleanings from pet rabbit, hamster or guinea-pig cages. You can even add your own hair and nail parings.

In general it is best to avoid animal remains. Three reasons. Firstly, they smell. Secondly, they tend to attract undesirable scavengers — cats, dogs, rats, foxes and so on. Thirdly, they take longer to compost than vegetable waste.

It is best too, to avoid woody vegetable waste. This, too, takes far longer to compost than other vegetable waste. Hedge clippings, for example, take on average, eight times longer to compost than soft green waste, like lawn clippings. So save woody waste for the bonfire. Bonfire ash has an important part to play in natural gardening.

Mistakes to Avoid. There are three mistakes people often make when they first start using compost bins. The first is filling the bin with only one ingredient — only lawn clippings, only yellowing vegetable leaves, only windfall fruits. The problem is that by using only one ingredient you do not get sufficient bacteria, or sufficient variety of bacteria, for composting to take place effectively. In time, if you are patient, the heap will rot down, but rot it will, not compost. Use as many different ingredients in your compost bin as are readily available to you.

The second is not to allow the compost bin to dry out. If it dries out the bacteria in it die, and the composting stops. Moral: check the contents of the bin in dry weather; if it seems to be drying out, damp it down.

The third is allowing the compost to become too wet for the bacteria to work. This is usually a winter problem. If you have built your heap on the updraft principle, drainage should be perfect, so you should not find waterlogging a problem. If it is a problem cover the bin during heavy rains. Use boards, or black plastic sheeting weighted down with bricks, rocks or heavy boards.

Activators. If you read your gardening magazines often enough, especially if you flick through the advertisements, or if you often browse around your local garden centre, you may well have the impression that the world is full of activators, and that you cannot run an efficient compost bin without the use of activators. All that activators do is speed up the rate at which the compost breaks down into humus. There is no need to buy or use manufactured activators. All the activators you need can be had for free.

The finest activators of all are animal manures — horse, cow, pig or farmyard. If you do not have access to that sort of manure, use cleanings from the birdcage, or from the family hamster, guinea-pig, gerboa or whatever. If none of these is available to you, you will have to be literally self-sufficient. Human urine is one of the finest activators there is. Preferably applied discreetly, not by the direct method under the heat of the noon-day sun in full sight of the neighbours. Somehow neighbours do not seem to like that. If you cannot work out a discreet way of getting the urine from your system to your compost bin, buy some dried blood. If you still do not think your bin is composting fast enough, dig around the garden for some worms, and introduce them direct into the middle of the bin. Take care not to let the worms dry out between digging them up and burying them in your bin: keep them cool and damp in a tin filled with fresh grass clippings or something like that.

Turning.   The purpose of turning compost is to let more air into it and so speed up the rate of composting. If you are making your compost in a pit turn it once every three to four days for best results. If you are composting in a bin standing on the ground, turn it once a week to once a fortnight. If you are using an updraft bin turn the compost just once, to mix the ingredients together, about a month before you start to use the compost on the garden.

Refining Your Techniques.   There are two techniques you can use to improve your compost-making efficiency. The first is temperature control. Bacterial activity is most efficient when the contents of your bin have heated to between 42°C and 53.4°C/ 140°F and 160°F. You can easily check the temperature of the compost with a soil thermometer: they are usually obtainable from garden centres, but laboratory equipment manufacturers are the people to get in touch with if your garden centre cannot help. The temperature that matters is the temperature in the middle of the compost. If it rises over 53.4°C/160°F take action to cool the compost. Excessively high temperatures simply produce a revolting, slimy mess – not good compost at all.

The simplest method of controlling the temperature in your bin – but it is one you can only use with an updraft bin – is a tight-fitting lid. This acts like a damper on a solid fuel furnace. Remove the lid to increase the draft which increases the bacterial activity which increases the temperature: close the lid which shuts off the draft which reduces bacterial activity which lowers the temperature. If you want to control your compost temperatures to this degree of nicety use a drum-shaped, updraft type of bin with no ventilation holes in the sides.

The other refinement is keeping the compost active through the winter months. Normally the bacterial activity slows down to a virtual stand-still because the bacteria cannot operate at low temperatures. Recent research has found that the one thing that lowers the temperature more than anything else is winter wet getting right inside the compost. The remedy is to cover the heap in winter. Heavy gauge black plastic sheeting is probably the best material for this, since it sheds water landing on the bin from above, while to some extent retaining the heat generated inside the bin, helping to reflect it back down into the bin. In a large garden it may be practicable to wrap the bin with straw bales which insulate it against cold from outside, or simply to make a bin out of bales of straw or hay, covered with further bales of straw or hay.

If you have a large greenhouse, spacious cold-frames, or some high outbuilding where you can make compost in winter then this is best of all. If you shore-up a corner of a cold frame and make compost in it through winter you will find it can raise the temperature inside the frame by as much as 10°C/50°F – though lower rises are more normal. You could similarly use compost to supply some of the heat requirements of your greenhouse through winter. This, after all, is how old-fashioned tan-pits worked, and is the basic principle of the hot-bed.

When Is Your Compost Ready?   Opinions differ as to just when your compost is ready for use. Perhaps the truth of the matter is that the moment at which your compost has composted enough to be used really depends on what you are going to use it for.

Technically compost is ready for use once vigorous bacterial activity has stopped. In fact bacterial activity continues at a lower level for a long time, but vigorous bacterial activity has stopped once the compost has cooled. If it has been fully composted it will smell sweet and earthy, having a light, crumbly texture and be of a very rich, dark brown colour. If you want to use compost for sowing seeds direct, for pricking out seedlings, growing-on early transplants, then you want your compost to be as well rotted as this. If you want the compost for general garden use, then you can use it earlier, and the final stages of the breakdown of the vegetable waste can occur in and on your soil. If you use it earlier you may still be able to tell the origin of various pieces of the compost: things like cabbage stalks and corn ears will still be recognizable, and there will be quite a lot of stringy, fibrous matter in the compost. No harm in that – it is all good food for the earthworms. If you want to use compost in this state for potting up plants, feeding the lawn and so on, simply sift it, and throw any coarse matter you cannot use straight away back into the compost bin.

How to Use Your Compost. Compost is to your garden what leaf-fall is to a forest floor. It is a natural mulch, and that is by far the best way to use it – simply as a mulch. You can dig it into the soil if you want – just into the top 10cm/4in – no more. Most of us have been conditioned into thinking that digging is essential to gardening, but it is not. You will achieve the same results if you just spread the compost over the land as a mulch 7cm/3in deep and leave it there. The worms will dig it into the ground for you. Certainly earthworms are far more efficient at digging and at mixing compost into the soil in a way plants can use than is a man with a spade. Earthworms work two ways in your favour: they bring valuable minerals up from deeper down in the soil and mix it with your compost, while they drag your compost deeper down into the soil. Their castings are particularly valuable sources of food for plants. Recent research in the United Kingdom has shown that a healthy earthworm can pass over forty tons of castings through its system in a year. Researchers in the United States of America have found earthworm populations as high as 1,500,000 per 0.4ha/1 acre in soils rich in organic matter. Just think of the mixing of compost and soil they can carry out. Unless you think you could do better, it makes sense to leave the digging to the earthworms. So use your compost mainly as a mulch.

Mulch every part of the garden. Mulch the vegetable patch before planting, use another mulch as a side-dressing in early summer, and use yet another mulch on the vegetable patch before winter sets in. Mulch beds where you grow annuals or bedding plants before putting the plants out and again after you have lifted them. Mulch all permanent plantings (shrub borders, perennial borders and so on) annually, either spring or fall. Mulch the lawn with fine sifted compost spring and fall, and mulch ground-cover plantings lightly every spring with more compost.

On open land apply at the rate of one barrow-load per m²/yd²: it works out at about 7cm/3in thickness.

If you keep on doing this year after year, year in and year out, you will rapidly increase the fertility of your soil, and gradually increase the useable depth of the topsoil.

Apart from mulching, you can use finely sifted compost for direct seeding, for growing-on your transplants, potting-up for pot plants, house plants and almost anything else you grow.

The Bonfire.
Always keep a permanent site for a bonfire, and use it to burn any waste from your garden that you do not think will compost properly, especially woody garden waste. If you have got hedges you will have plenty of woody garden waste on your hands. Bonfire ash is rich in potash: use it as a mulch, or use it in the sandwich in the compost bin.

If you are environmentally-oriented you probably know that smoke from bonfires is considered by some authorities to be as much as eight times as carcinogenous as cigarette smoke. They may be right. So if you are going to have a bonfire, make it blaze, get a red heart going and have clean sharp flames licking up into the air, then put it out with earth or water. Do not just let it steam, smoulder or smoke.

A Closer Look at the Earthworm.
I have already suggested that you let your earthworms do your digging for you, but if you want to grow healthy plants in a healthy soil, it is worth pausing a moment to pay homage to the earthworm.

Primitive tribes in Africa settle with their cattle wherever the worm-castings are thickest: they know the grazing for their cattle will be good there. Aristotle called them the intestines of the earth. Darwin figured out just what they do for the soil. Recent researchers have proved them even more valuable to soil management than even Darwin dreamed.

The topsoils of the world have been virtually made by earthworms. As they burrow they ingest inert soil and humus, and their castings are richer than either. A single earthworm casts its own weight in castings every twenty-four hours. They burrow as much as 2m/6ft down into the ground, and on a soil rich in earthworms a 5cm/2in downpour will disappear in fifteen seconds: it can take two hours or more on heavy clay with low earthworm populations. This earthworm activity creates a good soil structure, in which not only healthy plants can flourish, but also healthy soil populations. Worms are short-lived, though. Their life-span is two years at most. When they die their bodies decay into a remarkably rich source of nitrogen. All in all, earthworms can do more for your soil and your plants than any other single item – certainly more than you can do yourself. Liberal quantities of organic matter are all they need in order to thrive.

The English naturalist Gilbert White, writing in 1777, said 'that the earth without worms would soon become cold, hard-bound, and void of fermentation, and consequently sterile . . .'

Ironic then, that one of the world's most widely used agricultural artificial fertilizers, ammonium sulphate, is used by green-keepers on golf courses as a worm-killer.

5/Friend or Foe

Most gardeners regard just about any small creature that flits, flies, flutters, creeps, crawls, adheres to the undersides of leaves or otherwise threatens their precious plants as an enemy to be destroyed on sight. For too many people, the first reaction on seeing a bug on a plant is to reach for the nearest aerosol bomb. Some people even use these deadly pesticides as a prophylactic measure, spraying plants before the bugs even get there. For them the only good bug is a dead bug. Utopia is a garden in which there are no insects at all.

It is difficult rationally to explain the degree of abhorrence with which we attack the bugs in our gardens. It goes far beyond anything that is justified by their size or by the actual amount of damage they do. Perhaps our reaction is just a conditioned reflex, one carefully conditioned by the chemical companies and their ad-men: after all, this is exactly how they would like us to react every time we see a bug. Yet there seems to be rather more to it than that. Throughout history man's approach to nature has been the arrogant one of trying to beat or batter it into submission. We used arsenic and copper and all sorts of other more basic substances in huge quantities, and succeeded in doing an enormous amount of damage, long before the modern pesticides we invented or marketed. Probably ever since we started to cultivate plants we have been trying one active agent or another to fight our battle with the bugs. Possibly, too, our conditioning starts in childhood; most of us were told, when young, to keep flies off food — they carried germs. Such insistent messages of hygiene, drummed into us through the formative years of our childhood could have more far-reaching consequences than those who drummed these messages into our tiny ears ever imagined. The fly was not a threat itself: the threat was all those invisible germs it carried. They threatened not just our food but our health, even our lives; they were all carriers of polio, typhoid, diphtheria: you name it they carried it, and it could kill you. Perhaps when we are adults we transfer this fear, this sense of our survival being threatened, onto the bugs that attack our plants, especially if it is our food plants they attack.

It is quite possible that our aggression against the bugs is even more fundamental to our make-up than this. There is a current psychology theory going the rounds that we fear germs, bugs and so on, the way our more religious forefathers feared the devil: germs, bugs and so on are invisible doers of evil, the direct inheritors of the theo-motive concepts of incubi and succubi. Yet perhaps even Satan and his carefully ordered, numbered and recorded hierarchy of devils of differing degrees were in their turn only a rationalization of something still more fundamental to us as animals. Perhaps, deep down inside every one of us, though most of us are very unwilling to admit it, we know that, beneath the newly acquired veneer of civilization, and the even more modern myth of our industrio-technological mastery of the world, we are, after all, only animals, like other animals, and that, like them, we too are merely protagonists in the perpetual struggle for survival, that our moment of supremacy may be only brief and knowing that, perhaps even we, in spite of our sophistication and the super-resources at our fingertips, are merely mortal, not just as individuals but as a race, a species and that, like the dinosaurs before us, we could be wiped from the planet in a very brief moment of time. It may even be that some collective species instinct warns us of the dangers that lie in wait for us. It is the tiny, the minute, the microscopic we fear most. We can see if a bull or a bison rushes at us: we are never quite sure whether the intentions of very tiny creatures are for good or for evil.

There are precedents that justify our fears: the Black Death killed 75,000,000 people, reduced the population of Europe by seven-eighths and changed the course of history; the Bubonic Plague killed over 60,000,000 people in Europe. Nor are such disasters only ancient: the influenza epidemic of 1918 killed nearly 22,000,000 people. There are other, lesser disasters dotted across historic time.

The creatures that attack our food plants, too, have changed the course of history not once, but several times: wheat rust drove the Israelites to migrate to Egypt; ergot of rye, the dreaded 'holy fire' (and, incidentally, the source of modern LSD) destroyed the massive armies of Peter the Great at Astrakhan in 1722; Potato Blight in Ireland in the 1840s did much to shape the modern history of North America. In little more than the twelve months that spanned the summer of 1974 and 1975, Dutch Elm disease, a beetle borne fungus disease, changed the landscape of England for a hundred years to come, virtually wiping out all the elms across vast landscapes. Controls were available, but they were used too little, and too late. Seeing the amount of damage done in so short a time, it certainly is frightening to contemplate what might have happened had this been a bug that attacked one of our staple foodcrops – wheat or rice.

If it really is these secret, inner fears, the sense of the threat the bugs offer to us, both as individuals and as a species, that we react to every time we reach for an aerosol of chemical death, then we are reacting wrongly. Every time we spray bugs with pesticides we only bring the disaster we fear closer to us, make the probability of its happening more likely. It is like giving antibiotics to children for every cough, cold or sore throat: they become so accustomed to antibiotics that when they are really ill the antibiotics are useless. The widespread use of pesticides works the same way. Here is why.

There are over 1,000,000 named species of insects the world across, with new species being named every year. In the United States of America there are over 86,000 insect species: 76,000 of those are positively beneficial to man and his plants. Less than 1% of all known species of insect or mite the world across can be considered as harmful to us or our plants.

Even then we are taking a rather arrogant view of the world, a view that is entirely anthropocentric: a sparrow-hawk, a cabbage white or a slime fungus would adjudge totally different species harmful from those that we single out. We will never win the world if we assume that it is there for our benefit. It is not. We are merely one of the millions of species which live in an ever-changing interrelationship. It is these old attitudes that tempt us to think that the Utopia garden would be one in which there were no bugs. In fact a world without bugs would be a sterile world, a dead world. Certainly neither man nor the higher plants he loves so much, could exist without the insects.

Insects play a very important role in the world in which we live. Without them it is very probable that the endless cycle of life, birth, death and decay and recycling would cease. Good hard facts have been discovered by research workers in the United States of America that seem to indicate that without the aid of the insects the bacteria and moulds could not cope with the enormous quantity of dead plant and animal tissues that are for ever being recycled. The insects play a crucial role here, a role that is particularly noticeable in the tropics, but, though less obvious, equally vital in temperate and cool temperate regions. The larval stage of many insects, especially the larvae of ants, termites and many species of beetles, devour fallen trees, all sorts of plant remains, as well as a vast amount of dead animal tissue, which is later further broken down by soil micro-organisms, to serve as plant nutrients. The insects, having built their bodies out of plant and animal remains, themselves die, themselves become food for soil micro-organisms, themselves food for plants. Make no mistake: a world without insects would be a world choked to death by the accumulation of dead plants and dead animals.

The insects play other roles critical to man's survival. Many are great soil improvers – though their activities may be unsightly if they happen on your back lawn. They pull vegetable remains down into the soil, burrow through it improving drainage and structure, and bring up, often from considerable depths, minerals which would otherwise be unavailable to plants. Other species control the spread of some weeds. Still others control the spread of insects which, did they not have predators, could become a real rather than an imaginary nuisance to man.

The most important function they carry out is the pollination of plants. It is literally no exaggeration to say that the world as we know it could not exist without the insects. The plants that depend upon insects for their pollination are evolutionary co-equals of the insects. Their development has gone hand in hand across billions of years. Some highly specialized plants like the orchids could only have evolved simultaneously with the highly specialized insects which pollinate them. Look at any garden full of flowers and remember that those flowers could not have come into being without insects to pollinate them: and may not continue to exist if the insects that pollinate them perish.

The problem is that you cannot wipe out the insects you do not like, without wiping out those upon which you depend as well. Insecticides are very seldom selective. The tragedy is that it took the widespread use of high-powered broad-spectrum insecticides for us to realize just how many insects help us, and how many insects keep garden pests under control. And how much more effective they are at controlling those pests than we are and our puny inventions.

By and large those plants that do not like insects evolved means of dealing with them millions of years ago: the rest learned to co-exist with the insects. The pine trees, for example, have developed chemicals which keep most insects from attacking them: and the insecticide in a pine needle is far more chemically complex and subtle than anything man has yet developed. So far he has not even succeeded in fully analysing the chemical structure of the insecticide in a pine needle. There are parts of the River Amazon where no birds sing, and there are no insects. It has been found that where this happens there are concentrations of chemicals in the river so poisonous to insects that none survive. These chemicals have been manufactured by plants along the river's bank in self-defence against the insects which might otherwise destroy them. By and large, plants can cope with the insects which occur in their natural habitat.

It is only when man starts to interfere that things go badly wrong. To start with man introduces plants into parts of the world for which they are not prepared. If, by chance, an insect that eats that plant is introduced at the same time, the chances are that it will have no natural predator, so the insect will become a real pest to the plant. Even if a pest is not introduced with the plant, some bug will evolve a way of life to exploit it.

One of the realities of gardening is that if you cultivate a plant, you cultivate the bugs that go with it too.

One of the realities of natural gardening is that wherever you encourage bugs by the cultivation of particular crops, you also encourage the multiplication of their natural predators – and most bugs have natural predators. What one is trying to achieve by natural gardening methods is a balance between those bugs which destroy the plants we want to grow, and those bugs which prey upon them. In passing it is worth pointing out that, though people often use the phrase 'the balance of nature' – particularly when they are complaining about how much man has upset it – there is really no such thing as a balance of nature. Nature is not and never has been, presumably never will be, in a state of balance. There is only a perpetual, slow-moving struggle for survival between species. Some years the bugs that eat your beans will do exceptionally well: other years the bugs that eat those bugs will do exceptionally well. That is the way the world goes. There is no absolute equilibrium between all living things. So that, when one talks in gardening terms of trying to achieve a balance, it is only in relative terms. Natural gardening techniques tends to encourage the bugs that eat the bugs that eat your plants. Pesticides tend to encourage a whole host of bugs that are extremely difficult to get rid of.

There are a very large number of bugs that are useful to the gardener. They should be encouraged: in many cases they can even be bought and introduced into gardens from which they are absent or in which their numbers are very small. These bugs are your friends: only a fool would kill his friends – but if you use pesticides you will kill them whether you intend to or not.

Perhaps the most famous and most ubiquitous of the predator insects is the familiar ladybird, ladybug or lady beetle, call it what you will. It is quite a small creature, round in outline when you look down on it from above, red with black spots. It is a prime predator on soft-bodied bugs such as aphids, spider mites, whiteflies, mealybugs as well as on the eggs and larvae of many other bugs and on scale insects. If supplies of these soft-bodied foods run out it will turn to Colorado beetles, alfalfa weevils, corn borer larvae, potato aphids and bean beetles. What is more, ladybirds are remarkably good at their job. They pay a lot of attention to what is going on on the underside of leaves – a place where too many gardeners fail to look for trouble but where troubles all too often start. They can squeeze themselves into surprisingly small spaces – tightly folded leaves, right inside opening flower-buds and many other places which even sprays applied under pressure could not reach. Estimates of its appetite vary, but a fair average of the figures presented by researchers suggest that the larvae of the ladybird can eat up to twenty-five aphids each per day, while an adult can eat as many as fifty-five per day. What is more, the adult can keep up this consumption for several weeks. This may not sound very much, but if you have a population of a hundred ladybirds, they are going to be getting through over five thousand aphids a day, day after day for weeks on end. And that is sufficient consumption to prevent a plague of aphids ever getting off the ground.

Take care of your ladybirds, and they will take care of many of your problem bugs. Watch out for the eggs in spring. You will usually find them on the underside of leaves, and usually near a ready supply of food – such as aphids. The eggs are laid in clusters of five to fifty, and the clusters stand upright, the individual eggs being yellow or orange. The young larvae are alligator-shaped, blue-black, often spotted orange, though the spots are not always very noticeable. You will often find the larvae gently wriggling over the underside of a leaf, or on damp, slightly mossy pieces of stone or brickwork. Do not destroy them, thinking they are bugs. And do not touch them: their bodies are very soft and even quite a light touch will kill them. In the United Kingdom you sometimes find a second crop of eggs and larvae in the fall.

The closely related vedalia is a Californian ladybird with particular taste for cottony cushion scale, a pest which feeds on a pretty wide variety of fruits, nuts, vegetable and ornamental plants. In areas of the United States where cottony cushion scale is a real pest, encourage the vedalia: if it dies out because it has eaten all the cottony cushion scale, import some vedalias. You can buy them by mail order.

Golden-eyed lacewings, together with doodlebugs (or ant lions) are voracious general feeders. Their diet includes the eggs of many moths, thrips, aphids, mealybugs, whitefly plant-feeding mites, caterpillars and scale insects. A single doodlebug can consume as many as sixty aphids inside an hour, while the lacewings consume literally millions of mites or scale insects through their larval stage.

Even more effective is the rather somewhat intimidating praying mantis – which ought perhaps to be preying mantis. When young it lives almost entirely on two soft-bodied garden pests – aphids and leaf-hoppers. This is, from the gardener's point of view, its most useful phase. At maturity it enjoys a wider diet. It eats crickets, locusts, cinch bugs, tent caterpillars, many sorts of flies, these being main garden pests, but it also eats bees, wasps and beetles, which are not exactly garden pests. On balance its activities are beneficial. It is another biological pest controller that can be bought by mail order and released into the garden in spring.

There is another large group of beneficial insects of which most gardeners are completely unaware, mainly because, unlike most gardeners, they do their work during the night. These are the carbidae, a family of predator beetles, who spend the dark hours enjoying midnight feasts of such delicacies as cutworms, brown-tail moths, cankerworms and a whole host of larvae. Familiar members of this group include the soldier beetles, which attack the nests of webworms and destroy all the baby caterpillars: the Aleochara beetle, which, according to the United States Department of Agriculture (USDA) officials, destroys about 80% of all cabbage root maggots: the larval stage of the caterpillar hunter feeds largely on the damaging tent caterpillars and gypsy moth caterpillars: the rove beetle is a scavenger, feeding on decaying organic matter but seldom attacking living plant tissues. Fireflies eat large quantities of cutworms in their larval stage: as adults they prefer slugs and snails. They turn these slimy enemies of all gardeners into a delicious drink: first they anaesthetize their prey, then they secrete digestive fluids into them: after a while they drink the liquid which used to be slug or snail.

Apart from insects, there are many other creatures that feed upon the bugs that feed on our plants. Frogs and toads are particularly good destroyers of a wide range of pest bugs: thrushes and blackbirds destroy slugs, snails and several other nuisances, as do hedgehogs, bats and several other creatures.

Besides the predator insects there are also the parasitic insects, and many of these exploit as their hosts bugs that are garden pests. The predator insects eat their meal as soon as they find it. The parasitic insects work more insidiously. They lay their eggs inside the bugs. The larvae which hatch out from the eggs then consume the pest-bug from the inside outwards. It may sound cruel, but the modes by which the creatures of the world obtain their livings are not always particularly attractive by human standards. Once the larvae have killed their host, they pupate, and hatch out to start the cycle again.

Two of the most useful parasitic insects are both wasps: the chalcid wasp in the United Kingdom and the polistes wasp in the United States of America. The former lays its eggs in caterpillars of several different types, nearly all of them predators on man's garden plants. The polistes wasp is more choosy: it has a particular penchant for tobacco hornworm, and in tobacco plantations has been known to achieve 60%+ control. It also parasites corn earworm borers and armyworms.

Closely related in their mode of activity, and usually called parasitic, are a group of insects which are properly parasitoids. These lay their eggs on or very near their prey, seldom actually in it. The emerging larvae can readily find the food thus provided. Only occasionally do they lay their eggs actually inside the bodies of their prey. The larvae feed on the internal organs of their hosts, but are careful feeders: they eat in such a way as to keep their host alive as long as possible. It is only when they are ready to pupate that they finally eat the vital organs of the host, thus killing it. The parasitoids are probably best described as combining the nastiest habits of both parasites and predators. They start life as parasites, then turn into predators, killing off their hosts.

One of the most useful parasitoids is the ichneumon fly – which is biologically a wasp, not a fly. It has a remarkably long, strong ovipositor, and is known to be capable of boring through tree bark to lay its eggs in worm and larvae crawling under the bark. It parasitizes a wide range of other creatures, but is particularly effective in keeping down populations of oriental fruit moths and tomato flies.

A tiny wasp, which is remarkably useful to gardeners, but very little is known by them as yet, perhaps because it is very tiny, is the trichogramma. The grown, adult wasps are among the smallest of all insects, with a span of no more than 1/50th in. The trichogramma wasp increases rapidly, as many as three larvae hatching out of a single egg. The adults parasitize the caterpillars of a very wide range of moths and butterflies, many of them harmful to garden plants. Over two hundred species of insect are known to be parasitized by this tiny wasp, and as an agent of control it is remarkably effective, killing up to 98% of the eggs of its host before they can hatch and eat a single cell of one of your plants. Again, these tiny wasps can be obtained from breeders by mail order for release in your garden .

Obviously these predators are not quite attuned to man's wavelength. They are inclined to eat or parasitize friendly bugs as well as enemies, but overall the good they do from a gardener's point of view far outweighs the harm they may do by eating the occasional friendly insect.

The friendly insects mentioned here are just some of the hundreds of bugs you will find in your garden: if you look more closely into your garden the numbers may well run up into thousands. Borrow from your library, or better still buy, so that you can always have it by you, a first-rate book on bugs. Learn who eats what in the insect world, which bugs are friends and which are foes, and most of all, learn to recognize them when you see them. Any gardener who branches out into the study of insects will be doing more for his garden than he realizes. But it is a study in itself. This book can only touch briefly on some of the more commonly encountered bugs.

6 / Natural Controls

Before we delve deeply into the actual technique of controlling the enemy bugs in our gardens, it is worth looking a little more closely at just what we mean by 'control'.

The first thing that must be appreciated by anyone gardening naturally is that there is a fundamental difference between control and eradication. We have already looked at the fallacy of the utopian bug-free garden, and fallacy it is. Even if it were possible to eradicate every bug from the garden, it would be self-defeating. The garden would rapidly become sterile.

Sadly, it is exactly down that path that the manufacturers of chemical pesticides are leading a large, gullible and often unsuspecting public. As has already been pointed out, broad-spectrum pesticides do not only kill the bugs you aim them at: they are inclined to kill all the bugs in the neighbourhood too, friend and foe alike. Pesticides cannot discriminate between the one and the other. What is worse, their use brings into being new classes of garden pests. It really is not exaggeration to say that the mites which have become such difficult pests to deal with, and which have so much come to the fore over the past decade are, as garden pests, almost entirely the product of the chemical horticultural and agricultural pesticides industry. These pesticides wiped out the natural predators of many mites, and gave them an opportunity to proliferate in a way that perhaps they had never done before. Had the pesticides not killed their natural enemies, the mites could well still be rather unimportant garden pests. The rise of the mites illustrates dramatically just how pesticides, far from solving the problems which they are used to solve, simply create others. Evolution never stands still. Eradicate one garden pest and some other pest will find an evolutionary niche there to take its place.

A further problem of pesticides is that they do not remain in the place in which they were originally applied. Neighbouring areas also suffer. The sprays blow across garden fences onto neighbours' gardens. The chemicals in the ground are washed by rains into subterranean waterways and may finish up miles from the place of original application. Where the use of sprays is widespread, beneficial insects may migrate into areas where the still heavier use of chemicals has made it impossible for them to survive. In their place, your garden will be filled with yet another round of pests, different pests, each time round more difficult to deal with, demanding ever stronger and stronger chemicals to kill them.

There are, however, viable alternatives to the use of chlorinated hydrocarbons and other chemical abominations. It is only fair to point out to anyone who has until now relied heavily on the use of hard chemicals, that natural gardening techniques will take between two and four years to become effective. During the first year you stop using chemicals, possibly during the first two, you may actually find your crop-yields going down and your pest-incidence increasing. Fear not: persevere with natural gardening and you will reap the rewards for decades to come. The most important thing of all is this: once you start natural gardening throw all those chemicals away. And never, ever use them again. If you use them again, your two-year lag period starts again.

All of which brings us back to first principles. The object of natural gardening is to have healthy plants growing in a healthy soil. Healthy plants are far less liable to attack by pests, diseases or physiological problems than are unhealthy plants growing in poor soils. The first preventive measure, therefore, is to work on your soil. The second is to move or get rid of the plants which grow badly on your soil or in your area, or which, for reasons you may not understand, just will not do well for you. The third thing is to avoid growing plants in positions which are unsuitable for them. Grow a bog plant in a dry, arid part of your garden and it will always look poorly. Move it to a bog situation or get rid of it. If you do not have the right conditions for it, give it to a friend who has. If you plant a tender climbing plant in a hot, dry position against a wall of your home, be sure that it has sufficient water at the roots to thrive: if it is in the rain shadow from the eaves, it will be too dry for it. Plants in such situations are prone to mildew and even in hot summer in the United Kingdom to attack by greenhouse red spider mite.

An understanding of the role in nature of garden pests may help you understand the ecology of a garden better. Everything in nature has a place, a role to fulfil, and the role of the great majority of garden pests is to act as scavengers. In the wild their purpose is to keep down weak and sickly plants, to prevent them spreading their weakness or illness to other plants. Nature, if it may for a moment be personalized, hates weaklings: she does not want them to seed, multiply and increase. Garden pests make sure they do not. But the more weaklings you have in your garden, the more pests you will have. So do not allow weak and sickly plants to remain in your garden: they make a focal point for an invasion that could, in time, spread to your more healthy plants.

Nature also has her rhythms, and you need to understand these. Very often the scavengers come in their proper seasons through the year. Watch your vegetable garden in early summer: if you have been growing spring cabbages, you should have eaten most of them by now; the chances are you will have left a few standing in the ground. You will see that some cabbage white butterflies will find their way to these cabbages, settle on them, lay their eggs on them, and in time the caterpillars which emerge from these eggs will eat those cabbages till they have almost disappeared. The problem is that by this time you will have planted your next crop of cabbages, and the caterpillars will move onto these. By August that next crop of cabbage will be over, you will have moved onto the beans, and another cloud of cabbage whites will come along to repeat the process on the cabbages you have left standing this time. So the cycle goes on.

The lesson that emerges very clearly from this is the importance of garden hygiene. Those left-over cabbages should be rooted out of the ground and put in the compost bin. So too, should any fallen leaves from the cabbages, or come to that from any other vegetable crop. Fallen vegetable leaves act like a magnet to every slug and snail in your neighbourhood.

The next lesson to be learnt is the avoidance of mono-culture. In the wild plants grow in mixed communities, positively promiscuously, to use that word in its old-fashioned sense. It is possible, but often inconvenient, to grow your cabbages dotted around the garden, between the roses or the dahlias and whatever this year's fashionable bedding plants may be. It may be inconvenient, but you will have better, healthier, less pest-ridden cabbages that way than you will if you grow ten acres of them, as many market gardeners have to do. This is not to advocate growing your cabbages in quite such a promiscuous way: but if you want to grow four rows of cabbages, do not grow them side by side: separate them with other vegetables between them.

One way of separating plants of the same type from each other is by use of barrier crops. Though many horticulturalists look upon this as a newfangled and unproven idea, it was in fact widely practised in Elizabethan England, and as for being unproven, that may be, but there is increasing evidence that at least some of the combinations suggested here are effective. Try some of the following:

Chives or garlic between rows of peas or lettuces: this should keep aphids down.

Marigolds between hills of cucumbers, marrow, squashes or melons should keep cucumber beetle down.

Nasturtiums between rows of broccoli should keep aphids down.

Rosemary, thyme, sage, catmint, hyssop or preferably mixtures of these between rows of cabbage should keep the cabbage white butterflies away.

Tansy (a useful but little used pot herb) between cabbages should keep down cabbage worms and cutworms.

Tomatoes near asparagus should keep down asparagus beetle.

Chives between roses should reduce the incidence of aphids.

Other plants that have been found effective broad-spectrum insect repellents are marigolds, asters, chrysanthemums, and many herbs, especially anise, coriander and basil.

Barrier plants like these will never wholly prevent your crop plants from being infected: but they should vastly reduce the infection. And remember, with natural gardening you are not trying to eradicate all insects; only to control those which are a nuisance. The presence of a few insects, including pests, in a garden is natural. If those few offend you, here are some of the steps you can take against them.

These steps have been carefully graded. Always start with the least ecologically damaging. Only when that fails move on to more severe measures.

The first thing is to make sure that you deal with pests when their populations are small. Inspect monoculture plants (vegetables, roses) regularly through the growing season. Do not try to inspect every plant in the garden. Life is not long enough. Just keep an eye on those you eat and on any others that you either particularly care about or that you know are particularly disease prone. Turn the leaves over and look on the undersides. That is where most pest bugs settle first. They only show on the topside of the leaf when there is severe overcrowding on the underside.

If you think you have found a bug, the first thing to do is to make sure it is a pest, not a friend. If you are not sure leave it alone. If you are sure deal with it.

The simplest way of dealing with most pest bugs is to squash them between finger and thumb. If it is an aphid it will only leave a slightly sticky patch on your fingers. The problem is that aphids seldom come singly: they usually bring their families along too. So you need slightly more severe measures.

Try water. This well-known innocuous, colourless, odourless and theoretically tasteless and harmless liquid can be used with lethal effect against many bugs. Squirt it directly at the bugs under high pressure: use the hose or a spraying device. It will wash the bugs off the plant (often drowning them in the process) and onto the soil. Relatively few will climb back up the plant to risk your water cannon a second time. Apply the water cannon daily for a week, on affected plants. It will usually prove effective.

If it does not, move on to the next most harmless liquid known to man – milk. Use this in the same way as water. It is one degree more effective because it clogs the pores of the bugs, they cannot breathe and die of suffocation.

Stage three is to move onto vegetable oils: corn oil, sunflower seed oil, mixed vegetable cooking oils all serve the purpose. Use them in the same way as water. They kill in the same way as milk.

If you are not satisfied with these, try paraffin or kerosene. Again, squirt it at high pressure onto your target insects. It kills by the same means as milk and vegetable oils, but is more oily and rather more tenacious.

Washing-up liquids and detergents are just about as effective as paraffin. Add 1 tablespoon of detergent or washing-up liquid to one pint of water. Apply by the water cannon method.

If all these fail you, though they seldom will, you will have to turn to the ultimate weapons of the natural gardener. These are three materials that are all made from vegetables: derris, better known in the United States of America as Rotenone, pyrethrum, and nicotine.

Derris/Rotenone is made from the ground-up roots of the derris plant. It is usually obtainable in puffer packs, comes as a powder, and should be squirted directly at the target bug. Safe for man and pets: poisonous to fish.

Pyrethrum is the extract of a rather pretty chrysanthemum relative. It is effective against a wide range of garden pests. Never use it on any member of the chrysanthemum family: it will kill the plants. Safe for man and pets, poisonous to fish.

You will get best results by alternating derris and pyrethrum, rather than just using only one or only the other.

The third vegetable extract is nicotine. It is a very dangerous substance. It is deadly to man, pets and many beneficial insects. Only use it as a last resort. In the United Kingdom its sale to the gardening public is prohibited, so make your own. This is how. Simply save all the butt-ends from your ash-trays: if you do not smoke make some arrangement to collect all the office butt-ends. Dump them in a pail of water. Keep this at all times securely locked in a closet: be completely happy in your own mind that there is absolutely no way that children or pets could get to it. Dump the butt-ends in your pail of water and stir daily. Keep adding butt-ends until the mixture is dark, thick and tarry. Strain it into a bottle. Label the bottle clearly and keep it in a locked cupboard out of reach of children. Use the liquid in a spray-gun, diluted at the rate of one-quarter mixture to three-quarters water. Use specifically against specific bugs on specific plants. Repeat the application three times over a fortnight, then pour any remaining liquid into a deep hole dug in the ground: never pour it down a drain or sewer. Wash the bottle out thoroughly and store it in a locked cupboard out of reach of children until you need to use your nicotine spray again. Let us hope you never have to do so. It cannot be stressed strongly enough that nicotine should only be used as a last resort: it is deadly poison to man, especially to children, and to most pets. Take no risks with it.

If you have problems with fungal infections, use Bordeaux mixture. This is a copper-based fungicide. It is usually bought as a powder to be dissolved in water and applied through a spray gun. It can be used for seeds and seedlings to prevent them damping-off (which is caused by a fungus) and is particularly effective against mildews.

While these controls are effective in keeping numbers down for a large number of pests, there are other specific controls that you can use against some of the most ubiquitous of garden pests.

Aphids.

The prime enemy in most gardens. The presence of this pest in the garden can be greatly encouraged by growing plants in very dry positions, especially against house walls, particularly if the plants do not like such dry conditions. The first preventive measure is, therefore, never to grow plants that do not like being dry in a dry position. It is the old business of growing healthy plants in a healthy soil. Plants grown in organically rich soils seldom suffer from aphids. By and large the few that do turn up will not be much of a nuisance. Let them be: they provide food for the ladybirds, which later will prey on other pest bugs. If, however, you feel they are getting out of control, and they just might on your vegetables, this is how to deal with them. Take a small tin can and paint it the brightest yellow you can find. Fill it about three-quarters full of a mixture of 1 part washing-up liquid/detergent to 4 parts water. Either stand it on the ground close to the affected plant or hang it from a branch (if it is a shrub that is infected). The bright yellow attracts the aphids. They crawl up the tin and into the mixture inside it. This has a very strong surface tension, and it traps the aphids. Renew the solution from time to time. Another technique that is being found increasingly to be effective is the use of tin-foil as a mulch. Use it like a black plastic sheeting mulch. Just cut a hole in the centre of a circle of tin-foil for the stem of the plant, a slit so that you can fit the mulch round the plant, and cover the outer edges of the tin-foil with soil: the foil reflects the heat and light of the sun, and for reasons which have not yet been fully explained, the aphids just do not seem to like this. They certainly keep pretty well clear of plants that have been tin-foil mulched.

Slugs and Snails.

Universal garden pests, that seem to enjoy eating just about anything in sight, and are definitely partial to the one and only plant of its kind that you have gone to enormous trouble, not to mention expense, to import from the farthest corners of the globe. They just seem to know which plants you treasure most. There are several ways you can be rid of them: which one you choose will depend largely upon how squeamish you are. The simplest method is to sink a saucer of beer into the ground with the rim at ground level. Slugs and snails seem to enjoy alcohol, and they will come in their swarms all night long. In the morning you will find the drunk slugs and snails wallowing in their beer. Chop them into small pieces and feed them to the goldfish. If you have got no goldfish put the chopped up pieces in the compost bin. Another trapping technique is to place a roof tile on a couple of pebbles (boards or planks would do as well as the tile) and put some loose, wet straw, new-mown grass clippings or, possibly, some spare cabbage leaves under the tile. Check every morning and destroy whatever slugs and snails you have trapped. You can protect individual plants by taking advantage of the soft, highly sensitive bodies of both slugs and snails: a ring of cinders, sharp sand or slaked lime round a plant will provide a barrier few slugs or snails would willingly cross. If you do not want to dirty your hands with the carcasses of any slugs or snails you trap, keep a slug pit — a shallow pit filled with lime: it will burn their bodies up. Keep it covered except when topping it up with fresh cadavers, otherwise thrushes, hedgehogs and other creatures that eat slugs and snails may be attracted to it, with disastrous results. Never use slug pellets: if they are poisonous, the poison could readily be passed onto thrushes or hedgehogs which eat the already poisoned slugs and snails, and you do not want to lose them.

Millipedes.

The first thing is to learn the difference between millipedes, which have a thousand legs, and centipedes, which only have a hundred: well presumably. Millipedes are pests, centipedes are friends, so it is important that you know each from the other. Millipedes are smaller than centipedes, with thin, wiry bodies and multitudes of minute, hair-like legs. They are usually a dark chocolate brown (centipedes are much lighter in colour), and they have a way of unwinding like a watch spring and wandering slowly around the place. Sometimes they have red spots on them which centipedes never have. They are seldom a real pest in a natural garden with a humus-rich soil, but even so you will find them there occasionally. To get rid of them, take a tin can, make lots of small holes in it, fill it with potato peelings or something similar, and bury the tin a good 15cm/ 6in deep. Attach a string or a brightly coloured ribbon to your tin or tins, or you will never find them again. Dig them up once a week, take out the contents, which should include any millipedes in the area, and destroy them. Refill the tin and repeat the treatment till there are no more millipedes in the tins. How do you destroy the millipedes? Simply empty the contents of your tins into a red-hot bonfire.

Leatherjackets.

These are seldom a pest in a garden run on natural gardening lines, and even if you find them a pest to begin with, they will quickly disappear once the organic content of your soil starts to build up. Leatherjackets are the larval stage of daddy-long-legs, or crane flies. They are about 2.5cm/1in long, brownish-grey, tough skinned and leg-less. They feed avidly on bulbs, corms, tubers and roots generally. Any you come across when digging, chop up and feed to the goldfish or incinerate. The real cure is to add masses of organic content to the soil. They seldom attack plants growing in soils with a high organic content.

Cutworms.

Nasty little creatures these, cutting their way through the stems of many plants at ground level. They are grey-brown and various shades between that and yellow, about 4cm/1½in long, and basically they look like a soil-inhabiting caterpillar. Like leatherjackets, they eat bulbs, roots, corms, tubers and so on, and as with leatherjackets, the only real way of getting rid of them is to increase the organic content of your soil. Do that, and they will very soon cease to be a problem in your garden.

Ants.

It is questionable whether these could properly be called garden pests. They do a lot of good, certainly from the gardener's point of view. They are good scavengers, of both dead animal and vegetable matter, and their hill-building activities produce good, fine topsoil while below ground the passageways they open up improves drainage and air circulation. They can be a pest in a couple of ways. One is if they decide to build their nest underneath your rarest plant on the rockery/rockgarden. Their passage making activities can cause the drainage underneath the plant to become so efficient that its roots are left hanging in thin air, a condition which causes death to most plants. Their hill-making activities can be unsightly on lawns, and the improved drainage can cause quite extensive brown patches to form. Many gardeners curse them because they farm aphids for their sweet, sticky secretion, often transferring the aphids bodily from plant to plant. However, in rich organic soils there probably will not be enough aphids for them to farm. If you want to be rid of your ants, steamed bonemeal dusted on the nest, or pepper dust applied regularly, will usually make them go elsewhere. They dislike tansy and mint, so if you have any spare plants, put them right in the middle of the nest: the ants will usually start rebuilding the nest round them, but will soon give up and abandon it. Where ants are a problem in paved areas, pour paraffin or boiling water onto or into the nest. On lawns pour boiling water onto the nest. It will kill the ants, but the damage to grass will only be temporary.

Wireworms.

These can be very destructive in gardens run on conventional lines, but are seldom a problem in gardens in which the soil has a high organic content. The long-term way to be rid of wire-worms is to increase the amount of organic material in the soil. In the short term the most effective treatment is to bury pieces of carrot or potato in the ground: fix some string or a skewer to the piece you bury, otherwise you will have problems finding it. Dig them up daily and remove the wireworms. Then put the bait back in the ground. Wireworms are grubs, yellow-brown in colour, with short stubby legs and a dark head, measuring from 8-16mm/$\frac{1}{4}$-$\frac{3}{4}$in in length, and fat in proportion to their length. There is an increasing amount of evidence that *Tagetes minuta*, is an effective repellant and possibly even a killer of wireworms, and these can be used as barrier plantings between vegetable rows. They have also been found effective deterrents of the keeled slug.

Flea Beetles.

Most gardeners only know of these pests by the small, circular holes with which they riddle the leaves of seedlings, the flea beetles themselves being so small that you seldom see them. They are no more than 6mm/$\frac{1}{4}$in long, black or blackish, and beetle-like under a magnifying glass or hand lens. As with so many pests, they cease to become a pest once you have a high organic content to your soil, though even in gardens where there is and has been a high organic content for a long period, they still occur: it is just that they cease to be a problem. In the short term, while you are building up your high-organic content soil, should they get out of hand, apply derris/Rotenone specifically to the areas affected.

Cabbage Caterpillars.

The caterpillars of the cabbage white butterfly are a notorious destroyer of cabbages. But they are not specific to cabbages. They will feed equally happily on Brussels sprouts, cauliflower, sprouting broccoli, kale and are really at home in the wrinkled leaves of savoys, whose puckerings provide them with a safe hiding place. The point about these caterpillars is that they are one of nature's scavengers, whose main task is to destroy weak plants and prevent them from reproducing. In general they will avoid healthy plants, and fast-growing plants, their roots well down into a high organic content soil, will seldom be attacked. Seldom, but occasionally. If the caterpillars bother you, ask yourself, before you start wondering how to destroy them, whether it matters if they eat a few of the outside leaves? It does not matter much, since you will not be eating the outside leaves yourself, only the heart. What might matter to you is that the caterpillars, if left alone, might give rise to yet another generation of cabbage whites. If you want to destroy the caterpillars, the best way is to pick them off by hand, chop them up and feed them to your goldfish: their soft bodies are so attractive to goldfish they will practically fight over them. If you are squeamish, the alternative is to pour either fresh salt or salted water over the cabbages and their relatives. This will kill the eggs, and many of the young caterpillars too. The salt will not do the cabbages or their relatives any harm: most of them have been developed from plants which, in the wild, grow on cliffs overlooking the sea where they are subject to constant sea-spray. And the caterpillars quite definitely do not like salted cabbage.

Club Root.

This has become so much a pest of the cabbage family, especially in the United Kingdom and in continental Europe, that many people will tell you that you simply cannot grow cabbages without chemicals because of it. Do not believe them. You can grow cabbages in the natural garden. The first thing is to be sure you know what is meant by club root: it is all too often confused with galls of the turnip gall weevil, which does little harm to the plants. The galls of this bug and its close relatives occur near the tips of the roots, and close to the surface. If you cut one of these galls open you will find the small white grub of the turnip gall weevil curled up tightly inside it. Club root is totally different in appearance. It causes huge swellings on the main roots of the cabbages, making them gnarled, knotted, twisted, swollen and rotten. The smell is repulsive, into the bargain. The first steps to be taken are preventive. Grow disease resistant varieties where these exist. Never buy from the little man round the corner: buy only from totally reliable sources. Never grow cabbages on ground you know to have been infected with club root. And rotate your cabbage crops religiously. Do not be tempted to use chemicals here, even if you kid yourself it is the only place you will use them. This year's cabbage patch should be growing a totally unrelated crop next year. Besides, the damage the chemicals do in your cabbage patch will affect the balance of your whole garden. Remember chemicals do not stay where you put them and they do not just destroy the disease you intended to eradicate. Furthermore, nearly all chemicals designed to treat club root are acidic, and club root is primarily a condition of acid soils. Do not even be tempted into using the mellifluous sounding calomel dust: it is, in fact, a mercurous chloride: exceedingly poisonous. Lime is the real answer, together with a soil with a very high organic content. However, beware of how much lime you use. If you lace the land with heavy doses it will simply get indigestion, and prevent the plants taking up necessary nutrients. Slow and easy does it. Use ground chalk (carbonate of lime) at the rate of not more than 0.25kg/m^2 ($\frac{1}{2}$lb/yd^2) your first season, then drop to a 0.11kg/m^2 ($\frac{1}{4}$lb/yd^2) in following seasons. A regular application of crushed eggshells all over the vegetable area will gradually increase the pH figure, reducing its acidity. Do not expect instant success. Success in gardening is very seldom instant. If you find you get club root the first time you try cabbages, leave the ground clean for three years, gradually increasing the amount of chalk in the soil. Then try again. Never put infected cabbage roots in the compost bin: that merely spreads the fungus as you spread the compost. Burn infected roots. Some gardeners swear that interplanting cabbages and rhubarb, or even pushing rhubarb sticks into the soil between the cabbages will deter club root: the case is not proven, but it is worth a try.

Cabbage Root Fly.

Another ubiquitous cabbage pest, this attacks cabbages and cauliflowers, but very rarely the other related plants. The flies lay their eggs just below the soil: the maggots hatch out and head straight for the roots, which they then burrow into. Their mode of life is really a form of vampirism: they suck the sugars circulating through the root system, depriving the top growth of nourishment. Consequently the tops wilt, wither, and usually die. The most important thing here is to set out your cabbage and cauliflower transplants really firmly. This makes it harder for the flies to lay their eggs close to the stem. The next thing is to mulch the plants liberally with really coarse, relatively little

rotted, compost with a very high proportion of shredded vegetable fibre in it. The smell of the compost masks the smell of
the cabbages, and the flies look elsewhere for cabbages. It is
newly set out transplants that are most in danger. Strongly
growing established plants are attacked relatively seldom.

Parsnip Canker.

The secret of success with parsnips is to start with disease resistant varieties, and to make sure that the supply of moisture to
the roots is even at all times. Parsnip canker only occurs when
the supply of moisture is uneven. Obviously, in a soil rich in
organic matter the supply of moisture will be more even than
on a basic soil. What happens is that if parsnips get dry, and
there is then a downpour, the parsnips swell and split at
the seams. A miscellaneous assortment of fungi and bacteria
then get inside the parsnip through these cracks, and cause
ugly brown blotches in the root: in severe infestations the roots
may even rot. A soil rich in organic matter, a regular supply of
moisture and a good, thick mulch of compost, particularly after
heavy rains, usually prevent the trouble.

Potato Blight.

This is the dreaded fungal infection of potatoes that decimated
the population of Ireland in the 1840s and did much to shape
the ethnic destiny of North America. The cycle of the disease is
now well-known. The fungus first attacks the leaves. The spores
then fall onto the soil and move through it onto the tubers themselves. The infection can first be spotted when small brown or
black spots or blotches appear on the leaves. These grow in size
quite rapidly until the whole leaf mass becomes black, rotten
and smelly. The stems can also be similarly affected. If the
spores reach the tubers these will develop dark, sunken patches.
If infected tubers stay in the ground long enough, or if they are
stored in clamps, the fungus progresses until all that is left of the
tubers is a black, evil-smelling pussy mess. The disease is most
widespread in warm, wet summers, and is more common in
high rainfall areas than in relatively dry areas. The disease itself
is incurable. There are, however, ways of beating it. Because of
the cycle of the fungus, first early crops will usually beat its

appearance. The only way to beat the blight with maincrop varieties is to plant disease resistant varieties. There are many now available, and new disease resistant varieties are constantly being put on the market.

Onion Fly.

This is a real pest in conventionally run gardens, but offers few problems to the natural gardener. The grubs of the fly burrow into the incipient onions below ground, usually at the seedling stage, and feed on it, preventing the onion from ever reaching maturity. The onions usually rot instead. The main preventive measure is to avoid damaging the plants at any stage, but especially at seedling or set stage. It is the smell of the onions that attracts the flies that lay the eggs that hatch the grubs that devour the onions. Eggs are very seldom laid on sets: it is usually seedlings that are attacked, so another preventive measure is to use sets instead of seed. If thinning is needed, this should only be done in wet weather, when the seedlings will come out of the ground easily. Do not leave the seedlings lying around: either chop them up to flavour a stew or broth, or bury them deep in the compost bin – never leave them lying on the top of it. Always grow the plants in different parts of the garden each year. And do not be tempted into using animal manures to produce prize-winning bulbs, since this not only encourages onion fly but many other bugs as well. A soil rich in organic matter is all you need to grow bulbs of a size that will make your friends' onions look small fry.

Although this is not an exhaustive list of all the problems that might beset your plants, it does give a pretty fair idea of how natural gardening techniques cope with those garden pests for which those gardeners who live in their chemical fool's paradise simply have to use more and more lethal chemicals year by year. Chemicals are not the answer. A healthy soil is the answer. And you cannot have a healthy soil if you are constantly poisoning it with chemicals. The simple fact is that bugs generally do not bother to attack healthy plants growing well in good soil, when weak plants growing in poor soils are plentifully available and are, moreover, what nature intended them to eat.

Natural gardening does not mean that you will never see another pest bug in your garden ever again. You will: they always have their scouts out looking for weak or sickly plants to attack, and it is the scouts you will see. Normally, provided your soil is healthy, your plants will be healthy.

7 / Dealing With Weeds

Most gardeners approach weeds in the same way as they approach pest bugs. They are something to be ruthlessly eliminated. Any approach that is quite so crass can only be based upon a complete misunderstanding of the nature of weeds, and their role in the garden.

In the vegetable kingdom, all plants are equally plants. It is only man, with his infinite arrogance and his unending desire to categorize things and to polarize them, who labels some plants as weeds and others as desirables. If you make this sort of distinction, the natural corollary is then to label all plants which are not desirables as enemies. From there it is only a short step to deciding that the whole lot must be totally eradicated. The approach starts from the wrong premise. It might help to try to decide just what a weed is, and why it matters.

The traditional definition of a weed is a plant out of place. If cabbage seedlings were to come up in your rose bed, you would probably regard them as weeds. If self-sown camellia seedlings came up in your woodland garden you would probably nurture them, waiting expectantly to see how good their flowers might be. Though your approach would differ in each case, both sets of circumstances are the same. In both cases you have plants out of place.

Ralph Waldo Emerson came up with another definition of a weed, but one which still underlines the basic point. He described a weed as a plant whose virtues have not yet been discovered. Which is a very interesting definition. After all, most of the plants we cultivate either are or were wild once. They would still be wild had we not found virtues in them, either that they are edible, or that they have floral glory, or some other attribute that appeals to our sense of beauty or colour. It may be that, seen with different eyes, many of the plants we now regard as weeds might have virtues we should appreciate.

All plants are equally plants. The reason that weeds are a nuisance is that they compete for moisture, light and nutrients with the plants which we are trying to cultivate. Left to their own devices many weeds will quickly swamp the plants we are cultivating. It is always horrifying to see just how rapidly a once beautiful garden is taken over by wild plants the moment it is abandoned. In general, only established woody plants survive more than above five years dereliction.

All of this may be put into perspective if we look at weeds from an eccentric point of view. All of us have for so long taken it for granted that the removal of weeds is one of the prime jobs of any gardener: but is it? Is all this weeding strictly necessary? Could it possibly be that weeds do have a positive and bene- ficial role to play in the natural garden?

To look more closely at the question it is worth looking at what happens in the wild. Weeds, you would probably agree, are essentially plants of cultivated ground. Did they come into being solely and simply to exploit the ground that man cultivated? Did they evolve suddenly, in the mere 5,000-10,000 years that man has been cultivating the soil? They did not. Plants do not evolve that fast. The plants that we call weeds were always there and they had a very special role to play in the ecology of their natural habitats.

Take a landslide. It leaves bare earth on a hillside. The first plants to move in onto that bare land are pioneering colonizing weeds, usually ephemerals, tiny plants that take only a few weeks to grow from seed to maturity and seed themselves again, going through many generations in a single season. All are prodigious producers of seeds. When they die their remains form the first tentative humus in the new soil. These will be rapidly followed by the second generation of pioneer weeds, mainly annuals, which will first grow among the ephemerals but will eventually, by their more vigorous growth, swamp them. These second generation pioneer plants are things like groundsel, shepherds purse, touch-me-not and scarlet pimpernel. All are familiar garden weeds, and all are prodigious producers of seed. These will blanket the soil, laying down ever thickening layers of vegetable wastes and enriching the soil with humus: furthermore, they provide a green mantle, preventing the soil from eroding and by shading the soil, and also by the action of their roots penetrating the soil, keeping the level of moisture in the soil relatively constant. This in turn enables more permanent pioneer plants to move in, grasses and other highly seed-productive species. Once they are established the pioneer trees move in – birch, Scots pine. Later come the permanent forest trees which crowd out these pioneer trees, depriving them of light and being better able to exploit the food for which they both compete. In open woodland there is usually a wealth of plants at ground level, mainly grasses, bulbs and ferns. Above them are shrubs and under-storey trees. In addition, there will be many climbing and sprawling plants. The floor of the forest will be busy with animal and insect life: trees full of birds and arboreal animals such as squirrels. Below ground there will be a rich flora and fauna. In this type of forest, which is known as climatic climax forest, all space is occupied. All fertile soils tend to develop towards climatic climax forest vegetation. The very first weeds that appear in your garden are a start in that direction.

Two important points arise from this quick glance at climatic climax vegetation. The first is that nature does not like bare soil. It will cover it, and quickly. The second is that a certain amount of covering is conducive to the growth of future plants, supplying humus which in turn stabilizes the soil moisture content and prevents erosion, whether by wind, frost, sun or rain.

In garden terms weeds, while they can be seen as a threat – you do not, after all, want your garden turning into climatic climax forest – do have a positive role. They cover the soil, preventing erosion, providing a natural mulch of humus and stabilizing the soil moisture content. Many are positively beneficial in the garden.

Many weeds, for a start, can be eaten, either as salad crops or as flavourings in stews, soups and so on. Many others produce herbal remedies, condiments, drugs, while others provide food for birds and shelter for insects which are beneficial to the garden. Others are first-rate soil improvers: many contain nodules on their roots capable of fixing atmospheric nitrogen and changing it into a form in which it can be used by other plants. Even those that do not do this often improve the soil by 'working' it, their fine roots penetrating deeply, often working their way down earthworm burrows: when they die they provide organic humus. The action of the roots often breaks up and aerates the soil.

Many weeds are useful indicators of soil conditions. The type of weeds that grow on your land can tell you whether it is acid or alkaline. The death of weeds indicates serious soil problems – either the presence of toxic substances in the soil, or maldrainage. Changes in the colour of weeds indicate to the observant gardener incipient troubles which he can often correct before they damage his cultivated plants.

There seems to be a mutually beneficial relationship between weeds and earthworms. The weeds exploit earthworm tunnels, and also frequently exude substances from their roots which encourage the activities of earthworms.

There is also an increasing body of data which suggests that many weeds have a positively beneficial influence on garden crops, often increasing vigour, improving flavour or scent, and offering them greater resistance to pests and diseases. This knowledge is not new, though it does seem to have been pretty thoroughly obscured by conventional gardening practices. The American Indians, for example, to quote the classic example, used to plant morning glory among their corn plants. Early settlers thought they did this for ornament. Modern experiments have found that growing morning glory among corn plants increases the vigour of the roots of the corn. Such relationships should not surprise us. Some plants can quite literally only survive when growing in this sort of relationship. The importance of mycorrhize fungus in the health of a very wide range of plants is now well established. Other associations are being gradually discovered.

Nettles, for example, have a beneficial effect upon a very large number of plants. There are, in passing, several nettles that have no sting, and there is even a variegated garden form. Nettles are known, for example to increase the aromatic qualities of most pot herbs. They also make most plants growing close to them more resistant to invasion by insects, while their iron content is now known to have a deterrent effect upon the depredations caused by slugs, snails and lice.

There are many other weeds that are known to have a beneficial effect upon specific plants. The body of knowledge available on this subject is still limited, but is increasing all the time.

What is abundantly apparent from what we do know about weeds so far is that they all have a part to play in the overall scheme of things. This is not to suggest that you should have a garden full of weeds, merely to point out that in natural gardening the aim must always be to control weeds, rather than totally to eradicate them.

Weeds do need controlling. While many of them provide safe sheltering places for beneficial insects, many more provide safe sheltering places for undesirable bugs. The real problem with weeds is that they compete with cultivated plants for the available nutrients, moisture, oxygen and light. If more vigorous than the cultivated plants, they will ultimately either starve them to death or kill them by depriving them of light.

If you look at the succession of vegetation that covers the bare earth after a landslide and builds up to a climatic climax forest, it is obvious the weeds are primarily plants of poor soils. Their function is to lay down the layers of humus into which their more dominant successors can seed, root and thrive. The simple answer to weeds is to save them the trouble of laying down the first tentative layer of humus, by ensuring that you have a soil that is organically rich and by mulching heavily and regularly with garden-made compost.

It may seem too easy, too facile a way of dealing with weeds simply to assume that, since they are plants of poor soils, you will be rid of them if you have a soil rich in organic content, yet experiments have shown that this is substantially true. One of the most dramatic experiments in this direction was carried out at the Missouri Experimental Station. Two identical plots of timothy grass were planted. One was given annual and liberal applications of farmyard manure: the other was not treated. The treated plot yielded first quality hay, year after year. The untreated plot yielded poor quality hay, and quickly became thickly infested with broom sedge and tickle grass. Indeed, this so ruined the hay that the plot had to be ploughed up and reseeded every five or six years. The plots were side by side, both subjected to the same winds, to the same wind-borne seed, fungi and bug potential. Perhaps the most interesting thing to come out of this particular experiment was that the two plots created their own distinct lines of demarcation. Broom sedge spreading out from the untreated plot failed to enter the treated plot. The experiment was conclusive: what is not certain is whether in this case it was the density of the timothy grass in the treated plot that kept the broom sedge out, or the increased organic content of the soil that deterred this weed of poor soils. Other experiments seem to point to the second possibility as being the most likely.

One further series of experiments at the Missouri Experimental Station seems to confirm that it is the organic richness of soil that deters weeds. A six-year rotation scheme was worked out using corn, oats, wheat, clover and timothy grass. The control plot was not treated. The experimental plot was richly fed with farmyard manure, and the pH corrected and kept constant by the measured application of lime and phosphates. The treated plot remained substantially weed-free. The untreated control plot suffered constant invasions of weeds.

Thus the first rule for weed control in the natural garden is to create conditions in which weeds will not thrive. They are poor soil plants: create an organically rich soil, and they will be little problem.

The second thing to look at is the viability of weed seeds. Weed seeds have a quite incredible longevity. They will remain buried deep in the soil for centuries, dormant: but bring them to the surface by digging or hoeing, and they will germinate. Dig 30cm/ 1ft deep and you will bring up seeds that have lain there dormant since Queen Victoria or Mrs Lincoln were widowed, and they will germinate. Literally every time you dig the soil you bring up weed seeds and provide them with ideal conditions in which to germinate. So do not dig them up, do not hoe them up. Leave them where they are. Then the only weed seeds you need worry about are those that come in on the wind, or on the beaks of birds and the feet of human visitors. These can readily be kept under control by mulching with garden compost. A 5cm/2in layer will suppress all but the most virulent of weeds. Any that do germinate are easily plucked out of the loose, crumbly mulch.

There is another way of looking at weed control. What those pioneer plants of the bare earth on your landslide are doing is covering the earth in a green mantle. The earth's green mantle is precious to it. It does not willingly let it disappear. If it is destroyed it repairs it with a speed which is quite surprising. Seen in that light it becomes obvious that having bare earth in the garden, especially if the soil is poor, is to invite weeds to invade it in their eternal attempt to repair the earth's green mantle. So provide your own green mantle in the form of ground cover. This technique is easy and workable in many parts of the garden. It is ideal in the shrub garden, the rose garden, in gardens where there is an acid soil and you can grow rhododendrons, camellias, magnolias and so on. It can be done to a lesser extent in the perennial border, where plants can be packed so tightly that little else can get in. It is not, however, practicable in the vegetable garden, though the use of barrier plants and catch crops can serve the same function, though fractionally less efficiently. The secret of success with ground cover plants is to make sure that the ground is completely free of all weeds, especially of deep rooting pernicious perennial weeds, then to enrich it with a 10-15cm/4-6in layer of garden compost, placed on the surface and left on the surface. Finally, you must space your ground cover plants so closely that they cover the ground in a couple of years or so. Once established, ground cover needs little maintenance. It traps its own leaf-fall and any drifting leaves, so provides its own mulch. It will generally do even better if given a light mulch of finely sifted garden compost or leaf-mould.

Good cultivation, the rotation of crops in the vegetable garden, and regular mulching with organic materials will control most weeds. Finally, for some obnoxious weeds, there are barrier plants. Marigolds, for example, will effectively prevent the spread of bindweed, ground ivy and ground elder. *Tagetes minuta* is also an effective barrier against ground elder and celandine: some people even claim *Tagetes minuta* will actually kill ground elder, though this has yet to be proven. It certainly prevents it spreading, and if regularly planted will weaken the ground elder so that the ring of *Tagetes minuta* can gradually move in on the ground elder and eliminate it. Research is being done into other barrier weed controls of this type, but little that is conclusive has yet been established.

Thus an understanding of what it is that weeds are trying to achieve will help you to control them, just as understanding what it is that bugs are trying to achieve will help you control them.

Part Two/Getting Results

8 / Planning the Natural Garden

So far we have looked at the principles of natural gardening in rather general terms. The time has come to look more closely at precisely how natural gardening techniques can be put to advantage in the garden, in the vegetable garden, the rose garden, how they apply to a lawn and so on.

There are two aspects to planning a natural garden. The first concerns the physical layout of the garden; the second concerns the running of the garden.

The very first thing to consider when planning a natural garden is where the compost bins should be put. These are the heart of any natural garden, the humus factory, if you like, for without them, and without them running efficiently in a place where they are both easy to feed and easy to empty, natural gardening is just a nice idea, but totally impractical.

The prime requirements of compost bins are, as was explained earlier, the free circulation of air around them, and a position which should be in as much sun as possible and should definitely not be overhung by trees, nor jammed up against a building. In many areas it is illegal to have a compost bin either against a fence or against a building. It is worth considering putting an incinerator in the same general area as the compost bins, but not too close to them. You will quite often want to discard material that is not suitable for composting, but is ideal for burning, and these scraps can be piled beside the incinerator until you have accumulated enough to burn. Similarly you may quite often want to use ash from the incinerator in the sandwich in your compost bins. It makes sense to keep the two things together. It also makes sense to have the garden shed, where you can keep all your tools, in the same area. Ideally the shed should be of brick, stone or concrete construction: it is such a shame to keep burning down a wooden tool shed simply because it is too near the incinerator.

The area chosen should be central to the garden, so that organic waste from all parts of the garden can be taken to the bins without undue effort, but it also needs to be fairly close to the home, so that kitchen vegetable waste, emptyings from vacuum cleaners and so on can all be added to it without the deterrent of a long walk. On the other hand it does not want to be too near the house.

The best site is probably about one quarter of the way down the garden, and to one side of it. The whole area should have a hard base -- concrete -- since it is a utility area, or paving, either crazy paving or reconstituted stone slabs: the choice is yours. The whole area should be sufficiently large for four bins, an incinerator, the shed and still leave plenty of room to move around. You might also like to include cold frames in this area, and possibly, in one part of it, left unpaved, a standing area for newly propagated plants where they can be stood in their pots on beds of cinders or grit.

The whole area can be surrounded with free-growing shrubs, preferably evergreen, with hedges, fences or with trellises, where again the use of evergreen climbers would give the best cover. It is generally helpful if there are two entrances (or exits, depending on whether you are introvert or extrovert), one nearer the house, the other leading out into the garden. Apart from making access to the composting area easier, and saving wear and tear on paths or lawns, this helps to create a free movement of air through the area, which is very much to be desired.

The hedges or trellises, or whatever screening materials you use, could then be extended to make a division in a long garden, or to separate the ornamental garden from the vegetable and fruit garden. In very small space gardens where a hedge might be thought too unproductive to be justifiable, the area could be surrounded with oblique cordon, or fan-trained fruit trees. Although this will be seen-through in winter, its productivity will more than justify its presence.

In addition to the compost bins, provision should also be made for bins in which to store leaf-mould — and like composting bins these should be able to breathe freely — and for containers in which to store farmyard manure and so on until it is needed.

As for the general planning of the garden, there are a couple of points of importance in the natural garden. The first is to follow the time-honoured tradition of keeping the area primarily devoted to vegetables separate from the rest of the garden. There is a very good reason for this: crop rotation, though it has somewhat passed out of fashion since the introduction of powerful chemical weed and bug killers, is essential to the growth of healthy vegetables by organic methods. The other is that it is worth avoiding growing plants, whether vegetables, fruits, flowers or whatever, close to a hedge. It is worth going to quite a lot of trouble to avoid this evil, even if it means completely remaking the garden: after all, you do not have to remake the whole garden all at one time.

The reason for avoiding growing any plants close to hedges is firstly that the hedges, especially those most commonly planted such as privets, laurel, yew and beech, are notorious soil robbers. If there is any goodness in the soil at all they will not only find it — they will grab the lot. The result is that any plants you try to grow near hedges will be struggling for survival against odds which they can never win. They will be weak, sickly plants, prone to every pest and disease to which plant life is prone. And you will not beat the problem by increasing the organic contents of the soil. The hedge will use any goodness you put on top of, or even dig into the soil, leaving the plants as badly off as before. Apart from which hedges generally tend to harbour all sorts of weeds, pests, bugs and fungi, which can readily spread into your borders. The viable alternative is to grow your plants in island beds. Grown this way all the plants receive the maximum light, air movement, rain and goodness from the soil. Apart from which they look better.

When planting your garden it is worth taking the trouble to follow the traditional advice to measure it carefully and draw it all out to scale on paper with printed squares on it. It may seem a lot of trouble to go to, but if you do not, you will finish up drawing everything out of scale and distorting the dimensions simply so that you can fit in all the plants you want — on paper anyway. You will not be able to fit them all into the garden, at least not without severe overcrowding. It is worth remembering, though, that drawing the garden accurately to scale is something you need only do once. When you want to make changes in subsequent years, just lay tracing paper over your original. But make sure your original is right, and draw it clearly in black ink.

Just as important as planning is keeping records. This may seem a bore: in fact it is enormously useful. All you need is a simple card index. Enter any plant you grow on it, record how close you space the plants, and how they fare. If they die record this fact: if you know why they died, record that too. Over as short a period as a couple of years you will find that you can learn a lot by checking back on your records. You will find that some plants had a high bug-infection index because you planted them too closely. That others failed to fruit because no pollinator was near by. With vegetable and annuals record year by year the varieties you grow, the date you sow seed or plant, the date you harvest and, if you have time, the harvest yield – if you do not have time simply state whether the crop was good, bad or a disaster. Your garden is different from any other garden in the world, and it is only by keeping notes like these that you will learn year by year whether you are sowing seed too early or too late, whether you are growing the best varieties for your area or not, the right ones for your soil, and which plants perform best in your garden and on your soil. One thing you should take particular care to record, and it is something that may well not occur to you to record, is the density of plantings. There is a reason for recording this information. There is a direct relationship between the density of the planting and the incidence of bug infestation. In general terms, bugs will destroy more plants if they are densely planted than they will if they are well-spaced. It is a natural reflex. All the bugs are doing is thinning the plants, so that those that survive have room to do really well. If you space lettuces 5cm/3in apart you will find that three-quarters of them will be eaten by bugs. If you space the same number of lettuces 30cm/1ft apart you will find that very few indeed will be eaten.

The spatial relationships between plants matter, whether those plants are all of the same kind or not. The reason spatial relationships matter is that all plants enjoy plenty of air moving around them. Dense planting discourages air movement, and that in turn fosters the exponential growth of plant eating bug populations. It also encourages fungal infections: indeed, it is probably the greatest cause of such infections.

Two very important practices should be built into every garden plan. With the exception of the woody plants, all plants will do better if grown on a rotation basis. The rotation of vegetable crops is a well-established practise, but few people bother to rotate other plants. If you go in for bedding schemes, rotate the plantings. If you grow pelargoniums, lobelia and alyssum one year, use fuchsias, salvias and ageratum the next. You will get better results all round if you do this. Move your bulbs and perennials around too. Most perennials need lifting and dividing every three or four years to keep them vigorous, so instead of replanting them where they were, plant them somewhere different. Keep all the plants you can on the move. It will do them good, and each of them in turn will contribute something to improving the soil.

Learn what you can from nature about which plants grow naturally in combination with other plants. Learn more by observing the plants in your own garden. Make notes, for a start, of which plants suffer from the same pests and bugs. Note too, which plants have shallow roots and which have deep roots: they will make good companions. Note too, those which have nodules on their roots which fix nitrogen, and follow them with plants that draw heavily on the nitrogen in the soil. There is no short cut to your own personal observation of the behaviour of the plants in your garden as far as this goes.

Plan too, for barrier plantings. If you take over a property infested with ground elder, plan a programme of ground elder control: use *Tagetes minuta* in a semi-circle round the area infested, and each year close the semi-circle tighter and tighter on the ground elder till eventually you have driven it right back into the hedge. Then plant it right up against the hedge for a further three years, after which you may well find that, unless it is re-invading you from next door, you are rid of it. If it starts creeping back on you, use *Tagetes minuta* again. This plant is also effective in controlling ground ivy, couch or twitch grass and bindweed, all of which are difficult to get rid of by conventional gardening methods.

Also note plants that are incompatible. If you put two plants

that are surface feeders, and greedy feeders at that, close together, do not expect either of them to do well. Make notes of
which plants are incompatible, and, if you know why, note too
why they are incompatible. But do not assume that because one
plant is incompatible with another, all those plants are mutually
incompatible. You may find, for example, that potatoes and sunflowers are incompatible: and you may find that sunflowers
and pole beans are incompatible. The question is whether it
follows from that that pole beans and potatoes are incompatible.
In fact they are not, but it would be easy to assume that they
are.

Plan too, to optimize on plants you know to have a deterrent
effect on bugs. Garlic, for example, is known to be an effective
insect deterrent when planted among beans – so plan plantings of
that type.

Just as important as planning the use you make of the space in
your garden is planning the sequences of operations to be carried
out through the year. You already know that you can beat potato
blight by planting first earlies, and avoiding planting maincrop
potatoes. There are many other bugs you can beat by planting
early, but most of these will be dealt with in the chapter on growing vegetables.

Timing can be crucial to the prevention of all sorts of problems
in the natural garden. Hygiene, for example, is regular routine
activity in the natural garden: fallen vegetable leaves, tree twigs
and so on should all be regularly collected and put into the compost bin or stored for the incinerator. However, parts of the
garden, like the depths of shrubberies and the bottoms of hedges
tend to accumulate a lot of debris that is seldom collected in
routine hygiene programmes. Go through them thoroughly every
spring and fall, removing all the debris.

Early spring is when the bugs start their life cycle for the
season, and a few minutes each morning, or a slightly longer
period each weekend spent inspecting as many plants as you can
for the eggs of pest bugs will more than repay your efforts later
in the season. At this stage the eggs can be removed easily,
squashed between finger and thumb, or between tweezers if you
do not like making a mess of your fingers. Slugs, caterpillars,
snails too can all be picked off by hand and destroyed. Getting
rid of these eggs and bugs as early in spring as possible will greatly

reduce the numbers that you will have to deal with through the growing season ahead.

The seedlings stage of any plant is usually considered to be its most vulnerable moment to attack by pest disease or fungus. In fact transplant stage is perhaps an even more dangerous one. The plants are vulnerable anyway, being small, young and tender: they are even more vulnerable if they have suffered root damage in transplanting, and many do, even when the greatest care is taken to avoid damage. Transplants can receive a setback too, as their roots grow out of the growing mixture in which they germinate into the surrounding soil.

It makes sense to give these little plants extra protection, not only against weather but also more specifically against bugs. Cloches, tents, hotcaps all give some measure of protection, as do flower pots with their bottoms knocked out placed round the transplants, or even makeshift collars or stiff plastic sheeting, cardboard, (preferably waxed) or even little tents of linen, hessian or burlap. Some specific protective measures for vegetable transplants are mentioned in the chapter dealing with vegetables.

The timing of seeding and transplanting is also important in bug prevention. In general, the sturdier a seedling or transplant by the time the bugs get going, the less likely it is to be attacked by the bugs. It follows that it makes sense to get your seeds in the ground just as early as you dare, and to put your transplants out as early as you dare, the degree of your daring depending upon your knowledge of local likely last frost dates and whether you are prepared to risk loosing the lot by a freak late frost. The principle is a sound one.

If early season measures are important, so too are late season hygiene measures. In the fall destroy, preferably by burning, any infected or infested crops still in the ground, especially vegetables, annuals and biennials that have flowered. Healthy plants that are finished should go into the compost bin. It is only diseased or infested plants that should be burnt. Look carefully over the foliage of foundation plantings for pest bug egg cases that have been laid to overwinter: pick these off by hand (with the aid of gloves or tweezers if you like) and burn them: or feed the goldfish.

Finally, through the winter months, check all woody plants and remove any dead wood you either did not notice or did not have time to remove during the growing season. Dead wood is a potential source of fungal infection: burn it.

Planning your garden like this, not only in terms of the use of space but also in terms of the use of time are crucial if you want your natural garden to become a viable proposition.

9 / The Vegetable Garden

Different parts of the garden take on different degrees of importance in subsequent generations. If ten years ago — even five years ago — someone had told you that there would be an acute food shortage in your own country within your own lifetime, you would probably have laughed them out of court. For most of us, in the relatively rich industrio-technological nations of the western world, famine has for a long time been something that only happens to underdeveloped peoples in faraway places. Yet the fact is not merely that it could happen here, but that it is already happening here. Every time you go into a supermarket, some commodity you once took for granted is no longer on the shelves, sugar last year, bananas next year, coffee the year after that, who knows, but there is always a shortage of something, often a shortage of several things. The unacceptable reality is that we live in a world running short of food, protein and even the soil on which to produce food. In America alone, the self-claimed richest nation in the world, 2,000 people die of starvation every year. Hunger is not so far from home.

So long as our birth-rate continues to outstrip our food productivity things can only get worse, and we do not even seem to have the will to turn the tide. There is no need to labour the point: there is enough gloom and despondency around already. Food, after all, is like any other commodity. Scarcity pushes prices up, and food prices are rising. More and more people are turning to growing their own vegetables, but there is more to that than simply saving money or hedging against food shortages. There is a positive side to it too.

When you think about it, the criterion with which market gardeners have to live are not necessarily those most conducive to the best flavoured vegetables. What they grow has to be tough enough to travel, often hundreds, occasionally thousands of miles: it has to be able to look good even after it has been frozen in storage or stewed in the back of a truck. It has to look the right colour under the fluorescent tubes in the supermarket, and the longer the shelf-life the better. The varieties they grow have to fulfil these demands.

When you grow your vegetables you can choose your own varieties. You can select for home grown garden freshness: you may be in for a shock; you may find the vegetable so fresh, its flavour so unexpected after the tired old supermarket buys you are used to, that you think it is bad. Take heart: you will soon learn what fresh vegetables taste like. You can go all out for flavour, for colour, for size, for succulence – the choice is yours.

Almost anyone who has ever grown their own vegetables will tell you they taste better than supermarket buys. It may be bragging, and it may be psychological, but the chances are that the foods you grow yourself really do taste better.

There is certainly an increasing body of well-researched data that suggests that foods you grow yourself in soil with a high organic content and in a garden in which no chemicals are used, not only taste better, but are actually higher in nutritive content, than those grown with artificial fertilizers in soil where all the weeds and bugs are controlled chemically. Yields too, plant for plant, and row for row, are higher in well run organically organized gardens than they are in old-fashioned chemically run gardens.

There are four basic rules for success in the natural vegetable garden. The first is to build up a really good soil structure, rich in humus, of the right pH for the vegetables you want to grow and really fertile. The second is always to grow disease-resistant varieties wherever these are available. The third is to rotate your crops. The fourth is to maintain a strict regime of hygiene in the vegetable garden.

There is no need to run through the details of how you build up a good soil structure, and how you develop a soil with a high organic content. Much of the first part of this book was devoted

to that. It is worth remembering, though, that once you have enriched the soil you have got to keep on enriching it, otherwise it
will rather rapidly slip back to its original condition. You need
to keep feeding the soil. After all, every time you harvest a vegetable, you are carrying away from that patch of ground some of
the organic matter you put into it: so replace it. If you go into a
fairly open forest you will find that, apart from the loose leaves
blowing around on top of the soil, the actual depth of humus-
type leaf-mould is only a couple of inches at most, and it has
taken hundreds of years of natural leaf-fall to produce even that.
In the garden you have the advantage that you can add more to
the soil than you take out of it, and it is important that you
do so.

It makes such good sense to grow disease-resistant varieties
wherever these are available that it seems almost unnecessary to
mention it. Yet it is worth stressing, if only because there are a
whole range of vegetables for which disease-resistant varieties
are available, and yet many nurserymen and seedsmen go on
selling the older non-resistant varieties. Their only possible justi-
fication for doing this is that the non-resistant varieties taste better
or grow better or are heavier croppers. In some cases some of the
non-resistant varieties do yield heavier crops or taste better, but
this is becoming less and less the case. So much intensive research
and breeding is being done on disease-resistant strains that there
really is very little to choose between disease-resistant and non-
resistant varieties any longer. And even if there were, if you are
going to avoid the use of chemicals, you are inviting disasters if
you grow non-resistant varieties where resistant varieties are
available. It is foolish to invite pests and diseases into your garden
where there is no need to. Always grow the disease-resistant
strains when there is an option.

The rotation of crops is something that has very much fallen
out of favour since the introduction of potent chemicals, both
fertilizers and pesticides. If you grow a hungry crop on the same
soil year after year, you just double the rate of application of
artificial fertilizer recommended by the manufacturer. Most people do that anyway, so with really heavy feeders you may apply
it at as much as four or five times the recommended rate. If the
bugs become a nuisance you just apply more and more lethal
concentrations of already lethal pesticides. If weeds are a prob-

lem you just use some more chemicals to kill them too. And you just keep praying that the chemical companies will have stronger fertilizers, pesticides and weedkillers next year. And that is the basic philosophy of most of the people who grow your food for you on a commercial scale. And theoretically if that is what you do there should be no need to rotate your crops. So long as your soil lasts. But it will not. One day the crumb structure will fail, the soil will collapse, die, and blow away on the wind. And that precious topsoil, blowing away on the wind, is mankind's future as well as his past. It has taken thousands of years to accumulate, and yet with the type of non-rotation all-chemical growing techniques described above, you can undo all that in less than a decade. And neither the farmer who destroyed that topsoil, nor his children nor his children's children will be able to replace that topsoil.

The land that you garden is not yours to destroy. It was there long before mankind evolved and, if you treat it well, it will probably be there long after mankind has vanished. Your tenure of that piece of topsoil is as brief and trivial in terms of geological time as the falling of a single grain of sand through the neck of an hourglass. You have a duty to the land that feeds you, and that duty is to leave it better than you found it: not merely to conserve it, but to improve it.

In the vegetable garden, one of the most important things you can do that will improve rather than conserve your soil is to rotate your crops.

The rotation of crops is based on the very simple fact that different crops draw heavily on different nutrients. By rotating your crops all the nutrients are drawn on in turn, none too heavily, while your regular programme of mulching and composting will ensure that the nutrients in the soil remain balanced.

The cycle of rotation ration is based on four plots. In plot 1 you grow the greedy feeders – cabbage, cauliflower, kohlrabi, sprouts, tomatoes, celery, celeriac, cucumbers, leeks, melons, marrows, squashes, corn, spinach, chard, lettuce, and endives. In plot 2 you grow the light feeders – carrots, radishes, beet, turnip, swede, parsnip and other root vegetables. In plot 3 you grow the legumes – peas and beans. These are great soil improvers. Not only do their roots actually seem to work the soil, but also they have nodules on their roots which fix atmospheric nitrogen and leave it in the soil in a form that can be used by other plants. Many people optimize this benefit by digging the peas and beans after harvesting into the soil as green manure and, provided the plants are not diseased, this is generally a good practise. Plot 4 should stand fallow. In the old days it used to be put down to grass, or simply left for the weeds to enjoy. The problem there is that if you get weeds in the fallow patch they will seed everywhere else as well. There is an old saying that one year's seeds make seven years weeds, and there is a lot of truth in it. Modern practice is to use the fallow plot for divisions of perennial border plants, or what the Victorians called a 'reserve garden' – a garden in which the flowers are grown solely for the picking. The plants can simply be moved on to a new plot each year. If moved carefully and at the correct time of year they will suffer little setback. In fact, in the efficiently run natural gardens you can skip Plot 4, the fallow plot. The idea of having a fallow plot was to 'rest' the land. Natural gardening techniques relying as they do on the use of organic enrichment of the soil, do more than merely rest the soil: they feed it so efficiently that the resting period is unnecessary.

The rotation sequence, then, is to plant heavy feeders first in one, to follow these by light feeders, moving the heavy feeders into the plot occupied in year one by the legumes, and to follow the light feeders by the legumes, which gives a three year total rotation pattern.

One problem people run into with this scheme is that there always seems to be more heavy feeders to grow than there are light feeders or legumes to follow them. This problem can be beaten by dividing your vegetable area into four plots, two of which are used for heavy feeders. The sequence if you do this is to grow heavy feeders on Plots 1 and 4 the first year: then to move one plot of heavy feeders on to land occupied by the legumes, the other onto the land occupied by the light feeders. In the third year move the legumes into the heavy feeder plot of year 1, and the light feeder plants into heavy feeder plot of year 2. The important thing is to follow the heavy feeder, light feeder and legume pattern as closely as you can. Keep records so that you know which crops you grew on which plot in which year. Keep the record where you can easily find it, in the garden shed or the den.

The final essential rule is absolute hygiene in the vegetable garden. This means not only picking up every fallen cabbage leaf, but also the instant removal of lettuces that start to run to seed: the moment they start to run to seed they are ready for the pests, those scavengers of the vegetable world, to descend upon, like gathering vultures round a lame zebra. There is a saying among white hunters in East Africa that you never see a sickly zebra. It is true, you do not. They are the ones the lions, the hyenas and the Cape hunting dogs, the scavengers of that world always go for. The only zebras you ever see are healthy ones. Keep your vegtables healthy and they will stay healthy: they simply will not provide the pest-scavengers of the vegetable world with the food they need to survive.

Apart from the obvious things like picking up fallen cabbage leaves and pulling out bolting spinach, there are other essential hygiene measures which are all too often overlooked, even by experienced gardeners. For example, people all too often leave stripped sprouts stalks standing in the ground through winter, long after the sprouts have been picked. They are no earthly use there. They just collect bugs, fungus and all sorts of troubles. Their proper place is in the compost bin, chopped into short lengths to speed their decomposition. Sometimes these stalks are dug up and just chucked to the side of the vegetable plot. That is no better solution, possibly even a worse one than just leaving them standing. Another sin is to leave the haulms of newly dug potatoes just lying around on the vegetable patch in your eagerness to harvest your crop and enjoy the rewards of your labours: the problem is the old haulms tend to be forgotten, and to rot where they fall. At the least they may attract slugs and snails. At worst they could start potato blight. It is just not worth the risk of indulging in this sort of garden slovenliness: it is nothing more than laziness. Totally unnecessary, and equally unforgivable.

One very important aspect of hygiene, and one that is seldom mentioned, takes us back to the basic philosophy of this book, that of growing healthy plants in a healthy soil. Unhealthy plants are unhygienic plants. So make sure you do everything you can to grow the healthiest vegetables you can. Study the catalogues, study every book on vegetable growing you can, try to get the soil pH right for the particular vegetable you want to grow: if your pH is way-out wrong, do not even try it until two or three years after you have got the pH right. Study the types of crop available for each type of vegetable. Decide whether you want to grow spring lettuces or summer lettuces: and stick to it. Do not try growing spring lettuce varieties in summer, that is asking for trouble. Spring lettuces are short-day varieties: they bolt in long-day conditions. It is little details like these that make all the difference between success or failure in the vegetable garden. Study the water needs of your vegetables: some plants are heavy drinkers: marrows, squashes, gourds, pumpkins, cucumbers, all that group, will drink all the water you can give them. But do not try that on the eggplants: they will rot. What most vegetables need is a steady supply of moisture readily available at the roots. What they detest is first too much water then too little. It is evenness of supply that produces good, edible crops. A soil with a rich organic content, heavily mulched annually, will normally retain a fairly even supply of moisture at the plants' roots, but even so, watering may be needed. As a rough guideline, shallow rooting vegetables will need watering more frequently but for shorter periods each time than deeper rooting vegetables which will need a thorough soaking for several hours at relatively infrequent intervals. Typical shallow-rooting vegetables are lettuces, radishes, carrots, whose roots normally go down only 15-20cm/6-8in. Typical deep-rooting vegetables are things like parsnips whose roots, in good, stone-free soils will go down 1m/3ft and need a thorough soaking in order for sufficient water to percolate down to the roots before it has all evaporated upwards.

While water stress is used by some commercial growers to hasten crop production it is very definitely not recommended for the home gardener. It is too recent an innovation in vegetable growing, and too little is known about it. Most of the serious research done on it suggests that though it may hasten cropping, it can do a lot of undesirable things too. Some experiments with hastening tomato ripening by putting the plants under water stress showed that, although the fruits coloured sooner, and could be harvested earlier, some of the poisons that are typically present in unripe tomatoes, but absent from ripe tomatoes, were still present in the water-stress-hastened fruits. In general too little is known about water stress to try to use it for your gain. It could even be dangerous.

If you do not know what water stress is – it has not yet become a fashionable word – it is simply this. Most vegetables are annuals or biennials grown as annuals. In the seed trade, where the production of flower seeds is a major industry, water stress is widely used to speed the production of seed. Most plants, if they think they are dying, will hurry into seed, so that even if they perish, their progeny may flourish. One of the simplest ways of making a plant sense that it is threatened, is to deprive it of adequate water: give it just enough to survive, but not enough to thrive. Try that with lettuces and they will start to bolt within a week. Most vegetables will behave the same way. Do not encourage water stress: avoid it. If you find it is happening, you have done something wrong. Learn from your mistake.

Finally, most controversially but probably most importantly, use barrier plantings to break up rows and blocks of monoculture. Monoculture is virtually unknown in nature. Where it occurs, pests and bugs soon come to break it up and mix the species. Grow beans and potatoes together: it helps suppress Colorado potato beetle: use chives and/or garlic among lettuces and peas: it helps keep aphids down: mix white geraniums and/or odourless marigolds among any of the cucumber family, marrows, squashes, pumpkins and so on; it keeps aphids and cucumber beetle down: nasturtiums could almost be billed as the universal remedy: grown among cucumbers, marrows, squashes and pumpkins they keep down squash bugs and cucumber beetles; near beans they keep down aphids and Mexican bean beetles; near broccoli and cauliflower they keep down aphids. Potatoes and beans mix well, indeed they seem to have an almost mutual affinity, and a sort of mutual protection society against Mexican bean beetles and Colorado potato beetles. Radishes suppress cucumber beetles when planted among cucumbers, marrows and squashes: soybeans grown among corn prevent several corn bugs: tansy is an excellent foil against cutworms and cabbage worms when planted among cabbages or between the rows. Tomatoes and asparagus are one of the oldest of companion plantings: the tomatoes vastly decrease the incidence of asparagus beetles. As for cabbage white butterflies, the choice of companion plants is wide: you can use one, several or all of these, depending on your culinary tastes: hyssop, mint, catnip, hemp, sage, thyme, rosemary, nasturtiums, they will all deter cabbage white butterflies.

But all these are only aids. Ultimately you will only grow prize-winning vegetables, both size-wise and flavour-wise, in a good soil and by keen observation of the growing rhythms and requirements of the individual crops. There are no short cuts to keen, personal observation.

10 / The Fruit Garden

The fruit garden presents the natural gardener with quite a number of difficulties, one of the greatest of which is the simple, psychological barrier presented to most people by the belief that large, round full fruits cannot be grown to maturity without the use of sprays of various kinds, which is perhaps why the subject is so seldom raised or even mentioned in books on organic gardening or gardening without chemicals. Yet it is one of the most worthwhile areas for anyone wishing to garden without poisons to exploit.

Shop-bought fruits have probably been subjected to more chemicals than almost anything else we buy for food. Very often the blossoms have been sprayed with one chemical to prevent them from dropping and to help fruit to form, and then the young fruits, from blossom time almost until harvesting, have been sprayed again and again, sometimes at fortnightly, sometimes at monthly intervals, not to rid them of bugs and blights, but most usually to prevent the incidence of the pests and bugs at all: and even when they have been harvested the chemical processing does not stop there. Many of the fruits sold as fresh fruits have been sprayed or injected with chemicals to make them last longer once picked, or to keep their colour better, while others bottled, canned or preserved, have often been adulterated with still further chemicals to keep them tasting fresh, looking the right colour (even after cooking) and have had chemical flavourings added since their own flavours have been degraded in processing. Indeed, several of the additives of preserved, bottled or otherwise 'used' fruits have been banned, either in America or Europe.

There seems to be a widespread belief that you cannot grow fruit without spraying them with chemicals from blossom time till harvest time. This is utter nonsense. As with any other branch of natural gardening, so long as you have healthy soil, there is really no reason at all why you should not have fruits at least as healthy and probably healthier than those of your friends who use chemicals in their garden.

Even in the smallest gardens, some fruit can be grown successfully, but there are a few basic rules that must be followed. The first is that if you are taking over an already established garden and you want to run it without poisons, you may very well find that it is better to strip out any existing bush and cane fruits (trees are rather a different matter) and start again. Work the soil for three years, digging in all the humus you can and growing in the area where you want to grow your bush or cane fruits some crop like potatoes that really makes you work the soil and that do some working of it themselves. In general too, you will find it best to grow bush and cane fruits in a part of the garden that has not been used for them before, since many of the pests and fungus diseases of these fruits can remain in the soil for many years to infect any fruits you plant even after working in all the rich organic material you can. Lastly, if you find that you really cannot grow one particular fruit because of some disease that is particularly prevalent in your area, abort the scheme. It is a far, far better decision than deciding that just for that one crop you will let yourself lapse into using chemicals as a last resort.

Most soft and cane fruits have heavy feeding requirements if they are to set heavy crops of fruit, and they need an adequate and constant level of moisture throughout the growing season. By planting them in a soil rich in organic matter you are well on the way to supplying both needs. The high level of organic matter ensures that soil moisture levels remain pretty well constant, while the high organic content, particularly if it is topped up with regular thick, annual mulchings, preferably of horse manure, farmyard manure or pig manure where you can obtain it, but good garden compost where you cannot, will ensure the continued supply of nutrients to these essentially greedy fruits. This sort of treatment will often beat problems like big bud in blackcurrants that are supposed to be almost impossible to cure even with chemicals. As with any other type of plant, healthy fruit bushes and canes are far less likely to be attacked by pests and diseases than unhealthy plants, and more likely to be able to throw off any diseases that has already attacked them before you start gardening without chemicals.

As in the vegetable garden, strict hygiene is essential. Remove and burn all diseased wood: burn or compost all prunings. Keep the ground clean between the plants, except where you are making companion plantings.

Do not necessarily assume that traditional modes of cultivation training or pruning are the right ones. Watch the plants closely, see how and when they grow, note when pests and bugs attack them, and prune to optimize your chances of avoiding pests attacking your plants.

Blackcurrants.

Of all the fruits that can be grown in the home garden, this is one of the most worthwhile. Not only can it be eaten fresh or cooked, but the currants can be liquefied and the juice, kept refrigerated, used as a health drink through much of the year. It is one of the highest of all fruits in vitamin C – far higher than citrus fruits, for example.

Blackcurrants grow best on a rich, deeply worked soil with a high organic content. They should be grown in a sheltered position because, since they flower before they produce their leaves, and indeed rather earlier than most fruits, they should not be grown in frost pockets, since frost will damage the flowers, prevent fruiting and yields will generally be too low to justify the space involved. They should be sheltered from cold north and east winds which can be just as damaging to the blossoms, with consequent loss of fruit. Several modern varieties claim to be frost resistant, and up to a point they are, but even these will benefit from whatever protection from frost and cold winds you can provide for them.

Blackcurrants are normally grown as stooled bushes, and though this is the traditional way to grow them it may not be the best method for the organic gardener. The stooled bush technique calls for the removal of all old wood annually, in order to encourage the vigorous growth of new, fruit-bearing shoots. Not only does this system mean that the bushes have tremendously heavy feeding requirements – requirements which are not always easy to meet — it may also be one of the main causes of the spread of big bud — the prime disease of blackcurrants. Big bud is a fungus, and the fungus enters the bushes through the cut wood. Obviously sealing all pruning cuts with a pruning compound immediately a cut has been made would tend to deter the entry of bad big bud fungus, but matters are not quite that simple, as a quick look at any established bush will show. The centre of most stools is just a mass of dead stubs of wood where the fruiting growths of many years have been cut out. It is almost impossible to remove these or to treat them effectively, year after year, with a pruning compound, and yet it is these dead stubs, just as much as new pruning cuts, that act as a focal point for the infection of big bud fungus.

It is not without interest that in areas where deliberately culti-vated blackcurrants, grown on the traditional stooled bush system and heavily infected with big bud abound, self-sown seedlings, left completely unpruned, are usually free of the fungus and fruit prolifically. This has given rise to the practice of planting close together and simply allowing the closeness of the planting to force the bushes to make vigorous new growths. Very heavy crops have been achieved by this method. Grown in this way, the bushes can either be left unpruned, or merely pruned every six or eight years, which greatly reduces the amount of dead wood at the heart of the plant and, therefore, the chances of big bud fungus getting into the plants' sap flow. An even newer technique, though one not yet fully tested, but certainly one ideal for the keen gardener with little space, is the use of one-year cuttings. What you do here is either keep a few stock plants or buy in cuttings annually, plant the cuttings in rows and train the young growth flat against wires rather in the way raspberries are traditionally grown. Cuttings make vigorous growth their first year and fruit freely. The fruits are harvested, and the plants dug up and destroyed. The follow-ing year new cuttings are used, or alternatively, the cuttings may be allowed to grow on for several years unpruned. This technique generally produces more fruit from a smaller area than the tra-ditional stooled bush technique: it makes better use of space, and usually means that the fruit can be harvested earlier.

Blackcurrants, in common with most soft fruits, both flower and fruit when days are long and hot: the highest number of hours of drying sunshine occur at the time when the plants most need moisture at their roots. Provided the plants have been liberally mulched, this should not present much of a problem, but in exceptionally dry seasons it is well worth watering the roots of the plants before drought conditions set in. Manures, if applied, should be put round the bushes in winter, so that worms and rain will have had a chance to carry much of the goodness down to where the active feeding roots are when growth begins in spring.

Redcurrants.

This is an old garden fruit which for several decades fell out of favour and was little grown or known. Now, perhaps partly due to the interest in home wine-making, the widespread use of domestic deep freezers or perhaps simply because more people want to grow more fruits, it seems to be returning to popularity.

In general, redcurrants are frost hardy, easy to grow and the fruits are easy to harvest. The problem you are most likely to run into is having the fruit eaten by birds before it has coloured sufficiently for you to pick it. Blackbirds are the biggest offenders here. The options are to shoot all the blackbirds in the neighbourhood, or more simply cover the bushes with lightweight fine-gauge plastic netting. The latter is preferable since the blackbirds do so much good destroying pests throughout the rest of the garden.

Although hardy, the wood of redcurrants can be rather brittle, so plants are best grown in a position sheltered from strong winds. They should have a well dug, deep soil rich in humus, but do not need the heavy annual feedings that blackcurrants do.

There are three cultural methods of growing redcurrants. The most widely practised, probably simply because it is the oldest, which does not necessarily mean that it is the best, is to grow each individual bush on a single, short leg, about 15-23cm/6-9in tall, with the stooled bush on top of that. Left to its own devices a bush grown in this way will make a lot of vigorous, woody growth, and will sucker freely. To avoid the plant becoming a sprawling mess, which it can easily do, it is best kept to a mere 8-10 branches. On young plants it is wise to tie at least half of these to canes, partly to prevent the whole bush rocking loose in the soil under the action of strong winds, but also to help spread the branches. Pruning is done in two stages. The first is when the berries start to colour: the lateral shoots should be cut back to five leaves. The second stage is done in winter, when these same shoots are cut back to within half an inch of their base. At the same time, the growing ends of the main branches should be cut back by half their length. Treated this way, bushes should start fruiting within three years of planting. Suckers can be a nuisance with plants grown on this system: they often appear at some distance from the bush and can be very vigorous. They need to be removed promptly and completely.

The second method is to stool the bushes from ground level. Where this is done the plants throw up vigorous annual growths but do not make laterals. They tend to become very large and space-consuming, but will often produce heavier crops than when grown on the single leg system.

The third and probably best method of growing redcurrants is to train them flat against a wall. The system here is really only a modification of the stooling method. The canes are tied flat against a wall, and any canes growing away from the wall are ruthlessly removed. The branches thrown up by each plant should be trained in a fan against the wall. There are several advantages to growing redcurrants this way. They are easier to protect against birds, they take up less garden space, and they produce their fruits rather earlier than open ground bushes. What is more, there are records of redcurrants grown in this way remaining in perfect health and without any loss of productivity for periods of over thirty-five years.

Given good soil, well enriched and replenished with organic matter, in a garden run without poisons, redcurrants will generally remain free of pests and disease, though in some seasons some of the leaves may be slightly damaged by leaf-sucking insects.

Gooseberries.

Although this is not an attractive plant, having a sprawly, tangled appearance, and it is sometimes disliked because of its thorniness, it is in fact one of the most worthwhile of all soft fruits for the home garden. There are several reasons for this. It will grow as well in shade as in sun, and in small-space gardens can easily be grown under the larger trees. It is extremely hardy, and will withstand without complaint the worst that frost can do to it. But most of all it not only yields a heavy crop, but also one which can be picked over an exceptionally long period. The first fruits can be

picked when they are no larger than a pea, and picking can continue from then until the bushes have been cleared of fruits.

Correct cultivation is, however, important if the plants are to
be healthy and the yields high. The one thing gooseberries will
not tolerate is an ill-drained or waterlogged soil. Before planting,
make sure that drainage is good. If you have worked on your soil
as suggested in earlier chapters there should be no problems. The
soil should be deeply dug before planting, and plenty of organic
material should be added to the soil. Garden compost is particularly beneficial to the plants: farmyard manures can induce too
lush growth when the plants are young. The plants should be
mulched at every opportunity with fresh bonfire ash: what they
need most in order to remain healthy is potash, and bonfire ash
is rich in this, but it is in a highly soluble form, so that the ash
from a bonfire needs to be sifted and applied as a mulch round
the plants as soon as it is cool, and not left standing where the
rain can leach the potash out of the ashes. Given this sort of
cultural regime, the plants should avoid the several troubles to
which they are prone.

The most widespread of the disease to which gooseberries are
prone is American gooseberry mildew. This is a fungal infection,
and it has become virtually endemic to some areas of both Britain
and America. However, with correct cultural treatment, the
bushes can be grown successfully even in those areas. The fungus
first affects the tender young growing tops of the plants, so that
any method of cultivation which over-stimulates the production
of young shoots should be avoided. Hence the emphasis is on
potash, which promotes firm young growth, rather than on high-
nitrogen manures, which promote soft, sappy young growth. Any
young shoots seen to be infested should be immediately removed
and burned. The fungus spreads from the young shoots to older
wood, and in time so impregnates the tissues of the plants that
the fruits themselves are produced covered in mildew: as such
they are totally inedible. It is possible to nurse plants as badly
infested as that back to health, but it is a slow process and probably not worth either the time or the risk: the risk is that the
fructifying bodies of the fungus will liberate spores which will
infest yet other bushes. It is really simpler to burn such bushes
in a hot fire than attempt to nurse them.

Pruning is just as important in the control of this fungus as soil management. Pruning, incidentally, should always be done with secateurs/pruning shears for gooseberries, never with a pruning knife: branches are inclined suddenly to snap when you apply the pressure of a pruning knife to them: you might just fall over backwards in surprise, but equally the knife might slip and you might lose a finger or castrate yourself: it is simply not worth taking the risk. Pruning is best carried out in early spring, March in most parts of the United Kingdom and in the United States of America when the buds are seen to be swelling. The main reason for this is that the buds of gooseberries are much liked by birds: if you prune in autumn, they have only got a handful of buds to choose from, and they will probably eat the lot. If you prune in spring you can see which buds have been eaten and prune to take account of this. Pruning is very simple. You just cut back the tips of any long, straggly branches, and cut out any weak wood and branches should be encouraged to grow outwards, to form a basket shape, and any inward growing branches should be pruned out. Throughout the year keep an eye open for any dead wood, and cut this back immediately to the nearest healthy, vigorous shoot.

The other affliction of gooseberries is also a fungal infection, but a far less serious one. This is die-back disease, and it most often affects bushes that have been allowed to grow into a sprawly mess. You will usually first notice that a bush has been affected because one branch is bearing under-sized fruits when the rest of the plant is bearing fruits of normal size. Another first-line symptom is wilting of the leaves, and this can affect a whole large branch. Where you notice these symptoms remove the entire affected branch immediately and burn it. Watch for further die-backs on that bush and on those near to it, and watch very closely for the rest of that season and the following seasons.

Under proper cultivation the bushes should fruit well for twelve to fifteen years, before needing replacement. New plants can readily be raised from hardwood cuttings taken in autumn.

Bramblefruits.
These are not much grown mainly because, although the fruits are delicious, the plants send up long, unwieldy canes which require gentle handling since they are brittle and snap easily, and yet are so viciously thorny that they are difficult to handle at all.

Thick leather gauntlets are probably the best protection against the thorns. In spite of these snags, bramblefruits are worth grow-, ing, especially in the natural garden.

The bramblefruits include the cultivated blackberries (of which there are thornless varieties), and various crosses and hybrids, the best-known of which is the loganberry. All are usually considered very space-consuming plants, but this is only the case when they are grown conventionally along a fence. They can be grown in ways that use far less space.

Perhaps the least space using way of growing them is to grow them up and over a tripod or a four-pole, four-square structure. The canes can be trained first upwards then across the top of the structure and finally downwards, where they will mix with canes coming up from the other side. The ideal height for such a struc- ture is such that you can easily pick the fruits from the top of it standing on a pair of steps, or if you are elderly, from ground level.

Possibly the most useful place to grow them in the natural garden is on the fences or trelliswork screening the composting area. They not only make a good screen but also, because they are heavy feeders, will be in an ideal position to get a good mulch whenever you have any spare compost.

All bramblefruits should be planted in well prepared, deep soil with a very high organic content. Garden compost is fine, but animal manures are even better. The plants use a lot of food: they have to throw up long canes every year, and they also pro- duce a lot of fruit. Once established the bramblefruits should be fed heavily with animal manure in winter, and mulched through- out the growing season with compost.

Bramblefruits all produce their fruits on young wood, so the pruning regime is to cut out at the end of each season all wood that has fruited. This puts extra energy into the new growths. These growths will extend themselves throughout the growing season: they should be treated with respect: they will bear next season's crop. They should be tied very securely to whatever supports you are using, and the ties checked and if necessary renewed before winter sets in.

Bramblefruits all suffer from mildew if poorly grown. If you plant the fruits in well prepared soil and keep feeding them as recommended, you should have no worries of this sort. The only other cultural problem you are likely to run into is small fruit, but that is almost entirely caused by lack of moisture at the roots. In a regularly mulched, organically rich soil the moisture level should remain pretty constant, but it is worth watering in prolonged dry spells. Use cooled washing-up water rather than pure tap water or precious rainwater; it will not do the plants any harm.

All bramblefruits are easily increased by tip layering. This simply involves laying a growing tip of the current season's growth in a shallow trench in the ground, and covering it with soil. By the end of the following season you will have a well-rooted young plant ready to move.

Raspberries.

These fruits have generally the same cultural requirements as the bramblefruits, but need slightly different training. Their general need of a good deep soil, plenty of organic matter, and regular rich feeding, mulching and a high soil moisture level are the same.

The traditional method of training raspberries is to plant your stools 10cm/4in deep and 46cm/18in apart in a single row. Stout posts are driven into the ground at either end of the row, and at one and a half metre/five foot intervals along the row. Wires are then tied to these at 1m/3ft and 1.5m/5ft intervals. The young canes are tied to these wires as they grow. Once the canes reach to the top of the uppermost wire they are tipped (that is, the tops are removed). Tipping is a bad practice, since it deprives you of much of the fruit: a far better practice is to bend the tips over and train them horizontally along the uppermost wire. At the end of each season the canes that have fruited are cut out, and the new ones tied into position to fruit the following year. Many people leave all the young canes in position, but for healthy plants and maximum yields it is far better to leave only four canes to each stool. Plants should not be allowed to fruit the first year after planting.

One of the problems of growing raspberries is that they have a shallow but running root system, and unless you control the spread of the roots you could find canes coming up many yards from the original planting. Indeed many people have acquired their first raspberries by detaching canes that have come up in their garden from plants growing in a neighbouring garden. The only way to control the spread of the roots is to chop the runners off at a pre-determined distance from the rows.

In small-space gardens raspberries can be grown on tripods or on four-post squares, the stools being planted in the space in the middle of the posts. Three or four such plantings in a small garden will not look unsightly and will produce a surprisingly large quantity of fruit.

Grown under natural gardening conditions raspberries will not normally suffer much from pests or diseases. They are, however, among the most susceptible of all fruits to artificial fertilizers and chemical pesticides, insecticides and so on. The use of chemical sprays on raspberries weakens the plants and makes them even more vulnerable to diseases.

Strawberries.

These are probably the most popular of all the fruits that can be grown out of doors in the cool temperate regions of the world, with raspberries running them a very poor second. The trouble is that they are not only the most popular hardy garden fruit, but also probably about the most disease prone. This is no good reason for not growing them. For a start there are disease-resistant varieties available. Beyond that there are several different types of strawberries available. There are not just the maincrop straw-berries, which are the most disease-prone type, there are also alpine strawberries and, in the United Kingdom, the native wild strawberry: both of these are free from the virus which afflicts the cultivated maincrop type. However, one of the problems is that strawberries have been crossed, hybridized, back-crossed, interbred and inbred for so long that it is sometimes difficult to know which variety is what. As much as twenty years ago no less than 680 different varieties were being tested in one field at one horti-cultural station in the United Kingdom. Not one of them is still in general cultivation. The variety of today is out of favour or fashion within a couple of years.

In general strawberries are easy to grow well, but do take a little time and thought. They grow best on high ground: they fruit very poorly on low ground. Frost is the problem: late frosts, as late as May, ruin the blossoms: no blossom, no fruit. So if you live in a frost pocket, do not waste time on strawberries, or if you do grow them under cloches/tents. There have been suggestions that strawberries grow best on acid soils, but the case is not proven. What is proven is that they fruit best on soils with a very high organic content, especially soils in which the organic matter is relatively coarse and little decomposed.

Plants should be set out in well-prepared ground either in early spring or late summer. Those set out in spring should not be allowed to fruit their first season. Around May it is usual to put some sort of mulch under the plants to keep the fruits off the ground. Straw is the traditional material for this, but it has many disadvantages. Not only is it becoming increasingly hard to obtain, but even when you have obtained it and set it round your strawberry plants, it provides ideal conditions, especially in those parts of it which are in contact with the soil, for slugs and snails to flourish, and the only creatures which seem to have a greater passion for strawberries than human children are slugs and snails. Straw, though it has the advantage of rotting down and increasing the organic content of the soil, is not therefore an ideal mulch. The use of black plastic sheeting as a mulch has become popular in recent years, but slugs and snails flourish very happily under that. Probably the best mulch, though one that is not yet widely used, is shredded pine bark.

Unless you grow your strawberries in a wire cage, you will find that their attraction for wild birds is so great that your strawberry bed quickly becomes a veritable outdoor aviary. To prevent this, or at least to frustrate it, you must cover the strawberries with fine gauge lightweight netting as soon as the fruits start to form: do not wait until they start to colour – by then the birds will have had the pick of them.

Another of the problems of strawberries is that, to maintain good quality fruits, the plants need to be constantly renewed. Typically maincrop strawberries produce their finest quality in their first year, and their greatest quantity of fruit in their second year. They should therefore be discarded and replaced after their second or third year of fruiting.

Plants are easily propagated. The plants push out runners, at the end of which little plantlets form. If these are pegged down into pots set in the ground, severed from the parent plant once established, they will be ready to replace one generation at the end of a year. Only peg down as many plants as you think you are going to need. Cut the other runners off: they all take energy from the parent plant that could be put into fruiting. If you are growing plants on a three year system, you need four rows of plants. The first is first-year quality fruit: the second is bumper crop year: the third is end crop. The fourth row is the one into which young plants will be set. The next year they will be year one quality plants, and the third year row will have been stripped out to be replanted with ex-pots offsets. If you want to change varieties, simply put the new plants in the new plant row and replace the rest of the crop from there.

Maincrop varieties tend to suffer from a greenfly-borne virus infection. If this becomes a real problem the wisest course is to strip out the maincrop varieties and grow a different type of strawberry for three or four years. Alternatives would be perpetual-fruiting types, which you propagate by division, or wild or alpine strawberries, which are not prone to the virus.

Since slugs and snails can be a problem in the strawberry bed it is worth making traps for them in and around the bed. Saucers of beer are particularly recommended for use here: slugs and snails are not only gluttons: they like a good drink too, but they cannot hold their drink, and can easily be fished out of the saucer in the morning and destroyed while in a drunken stupor.

Apples.

Far too many people with small gardens do not grow apples because of the very out-of-date and yet persistent idea that apples make big trees; others avoid growing them because they cannot work out the complications of pollinators, while others simply become beflummoxed at the mere thought of all the different rootstocks now available.

These are all, in their way, valid excuses for anyone who does not want to grow apples. The simple fact is that anyone who does want to grow apples can simply go to their local garden centre and find out not only what is what and why, but which varieties and rootstocks are best for their area. And though this may well sound like a facile way of passing the buck, it is not. Different varieties and different rootstocks do best in different rainfall levels. For example, although you can grow a good cooking apple almost anywhere, it is difficult to grow a good eating apple in areas where the rainfall is over 100cm/40in a year. Your local nurseryman or garden centre will know your local conditions, both of soil and climate, and which varieties will do best in your area. It is his job to know, so take his advice.

In a small-space garden the best way of growing apples is either espaliered or as oblique cordons. Both of these techniques use plants grown on dwarfing rootstocks, and give the highest possible yield from the smallest possible space. Espaliered plants can either be grown on a wall, a fence or as a screen within the garden, and oblique cordons are ideal for fences or walls. Very high yields can be obtained by growing either trained shape against a warm wall, preferably one facing south or west, but if apples are grown against a wall the stem should be planted at least a foot from the wall, otherwise it will be in the rain-shadow, and the plants will not get enough moisture to grow well.

Natural gardening techniques for growing apples do not differ substantially from normal practices, although obviously there is no need to spray healthy trees growing in healthy soil. The most important thing is to plant herbs between the trees, especially chives, garlic, thyme and hyssop, since these will do much to keep down the incidence of bugs which might otherwise be trouble-some.

Pears.

These fruits take far longer to come into heavy cropping than apples, but there are other factors against them too. Although a native of Europe, including Britain, they are not well suited to the British climate, and really only do well in warm sheltered gardens. The main problem is that the fruits do not ripen fully on the trees before the first frosts, and few gardeners bother to pick and ripen the fruit indoors. Fireblight is a fungal infection which makes growing pears almost impossible in some areas, and there is no effective treatment or cure for this disease.

If you want to grow pears, choose a warm, sunny wall and plant espaliered, cordon trained or dwarf pyramid trees. General culti-vation is as for apples, though it is worth putting netting over the ripening fruits to prevent bird damage.

Plums.

The cultivated plums are all members of the huge genus *Prunus* which includes the flowering cherries, as well as plums, almonds, peaches, damsons and gages.

The biggest problem facing anyone trying to grow these fruits without using chemicals is the notorious and now almost ubiquitous silver leaf disease. This is a fungus infection, and as such prevention is possible, but cure is unlikely. The fungus gains entry to the trees through wounds made in the wood. It does not have to be a large wound, such as that made by the removal of a whole branch: a small scab made in the bark is enough. For this reason great care should be taken in handling the trees at all times, and pruning should only be done in early summer when the tree is in active and vigorous growth. If it is done at this time the tree will exude a sticky resin which will very rapidly harden to form a barrier through which the fungus cannot penetrate. If, as a result, for example, of losing a branch through a gale or through exceptionally heavy cropping, it becomes necessary to make cuts at any other time, however large, however small, these should immediately be painted over with a commercial pruning compound. The other important thing to appreciate about the fungus is that it can only fructify on dead wood. So keep your plums clean of dead wood at all times. Always watch for a dead twig: it takes only a tiny amount of fungus to fructify on a dead twig and yet a whole orchard can be infected from the fructifications on that one twig. So always remove dead wood as soon as you see it.

In general plums are open ground plants, not readily amenable to espalier or cordon training, and needing frequent root pruning if grown against a wall. Unless you have the room to grow plums as trees or bushes, leave them to others who do have the room.

Cherries.
Cherries, like plums, are in general, only happy when allowed to grow in open ground. The majority make large plants, and have vigorous root-systems. The only type really suitable for growing against a wall, and these will even grow against north wall, are the sour cherries — the cooking type, of which the Morello is probably the best known and the most widely planted. It needs a good depth of soil to do well, and the same precautions against silver leaf fungus should be taken as for plums. The sour cherries are self-fertile: the sweet cherries need pollinators.

Peaches, Apricots and Nectarines.
These delectable fruits can be grown successfully against a warm

wall in all but the coldest areas. Buy fan-trained trees to start with, plant them in good soil containing plenty of organic matter, but put a paving slab 1m/3ft down in the ground to prevent the plants sending down a tap root. You will need to take the same precautions against silver leaf fungus as for plums. In addition, it will pay you to put muslin or net curtains over the plants at night once the blossom buds appear, and to keep doing this at night until the blossoms are over, whenever frosts threaten, since if the frosts destroy the blooms you will not get any fruits. Later in the season it is essential to put lightweight fine-gauge netting over the plants to protect the fruits from birds. Underplant with herbs as recommended for apples to reduce the incidence of pests and diseases.

It really is quite surprising just how many different types of fruit can be grown in even quite a small garden. Although there is not a lot specifically that organic gardening can do to prevent pests and disease problems with fruits, the general rule that a healthy plant in a healthy soil is less likely to suffer attack holds good. The few specific preventive actions the natural gardener can take are all well worth while.

11 / The Ornamental Garden

The ornamental garden, for the purposes of this book, embraces those parts of the garden which are not solely devoted to either vegetables, fruits or roses. There is no reason, on the other hand, why both fruits and vegetables should not be grown in the ornamental garden: fruits can be used for hedging and many vegetables have highly decorative qualities which can add greatly to the charm of flower and mixed borders. The distinction is, perhaps, better made between the useful garden (in which fruits and vegetables are the main plants) and the frivolous garden in which mainly ornamental plants are grown: indeed, in an age when the world is running short of food, the growing of ornamental plants is a luxury in which we, as a species, may not be able to indulge much longer. On the other hand, a garden without ornamental plants, without the joy of flowers and the contrast of leaves, would be a drab and sorry garden indeed.

The basic principles of natural gardening do not change whether you are growing cabbages or chrysanthemums, apples or asters. The fundamental, underlying principles of natural gardening is to have healthy plants growing in a healthy soil, and a healthy soil is one rich in organic matter, well drained and yet moisture-retentive. However simple all this may sound in theory, one can run into minor snags, though most of these can be overcome by the application of a small mulch of commonsense -- an invaluable commodity in any garden.

Most of the problems concern the application of mulches of compost or animal manures. A typical problem is where one has a substantial area set down to heathers, a ton of well-rotted compost which one feels ought to be fed to the heathers, but one does not quite know how to set about it. The poor old heathers need their mulch: they have not been mulched for three years, but how do you do it? Plainly if you simply dump a ton of compost over the heathers they will be suppressed as effectively as any weeds by the mulch. The answer is that you sift the mulch very finely, spread it lightly over the heathers, and then work it in gently with your fingers, if the patch is small, or with a besom over a larger area. The secret is really to mulch little and often, rather than try to put huge quantities on all at one time.

Another quite common problem is where shrubberies need mulching but there is never quite a right moment to mulch them because you have autumn crocuses in flower throughout autumn until the earliest cyclamen start flowering, perhaps together with snowdrops whose season extends from late October until April, and these bulbs are followed by spring crocuses, cyclamen, and an assortment of daffodils. There may be cultivated bluebells or other woodland bulbs under the shrubs throughout summer, and of course it is possible by a careful selection of species to have cyclamen in flower throughout the year, and that means in leaf throughout the year as well. In a border like this, where the bulbs have naturalized, as they should readily in good soil, there is no time when they are out of leaf or out of flower, and so really there is no time when you can mulch safely. The answer is to apply the mulch in succession or on a sort of rotational basis, applying it only to those areas where the bulbs are not actually showing at any given time, and to keep on doing this: throughout the year the whole bed should get mulched, if only a patch at a time.

The natural ornamental garden should be planned and created on a soil that has been enriched with copious quantities of compost, leaf-mould or manure, depending on the type of plants you are growing. Consideration should be given at the planning stage to the type of garden you are going to have. If you live on an acid soil and want to put quite large areas down to camellias, rhododendrons, magnolias and other acid-loving plants, take care not to use any bulky organic materials that may contain lime. If, at the same time, you want to grow vegetables, make sure that the vegetable patch is downhill from the area in which you are growing the lime-hating plants. If it is above the rhododendrons/

camellia/magnolia area you will find that lime from the veg-etable garden will seep downhill into the acid-plants patch, and cause serious problems with them. If, on the other hand, you are living on a chalky soil your main shrubs will be the *Viburnums*, the tree paeonies and one or two other extremely choice plants, but the bulk of your ornamental planting will be of perennial subjects and bulbs: in which case you can scarcely add enough bulky or organic material: the more the better. On very shallow chalk soils you might be wiser to opt for a Mediterranean type of garden, relying largely for your effect on foliage plants, especially silvers, greys, and bold foliage plants, like agaves, yuccas and phormiums, with an abundance of all those exotic late-summer flowering bulbs that like a good ripening – bulbs like nerines, amaryllis, pancratiums and so on. If this is the sort of garden you want to make, your drainage must be perfect, but bulky organic materials may not be the best way of achieving this. For this type of almost subtropical gardening it is often more important to in-corporate large quantities of sharp sand and grit than to add too much organic matter.

If you want to grow healthy ornamental plants it is essential that you suit the type of plant you grow to the soil and conditions that are basic to your garden. The addition of bulky organic matter will improve any type of soil, but it will never change its fundamental nature: it will never turn an acutely acid soil into a alkaline one, nor will it turn a pure chalk soil into one sufficiently acid to grow rhododendrons and camellias. There are two main reasons for this: the first is that the acidity or alkalinity of the soil will be largely determined by the mineral particles in it: the other is that, however much you treat your own patch to change the pH the way you want, there is virtually nothing you can do to change the nature of the surrounding landscape, and water from around your garden will drain into your land, constantly reversing whatever changes to the pH you succeed in making. It is relatively easy to change a neutral soil towards either acid or alkaline, but even then it needs constant feeding with the right materials to keep it at the desired pH level.

In most ornamental gardens there is a combination to varying degrees of trees, shrubs, bulbs and perennials, often with bedding schemes for an added blaze of colour. It may just be happy chance that most gardens combine most of the plants, but it seems more likely that some fundamental instinct leads us to garden this way. It is, after all, exactly how a climatic climax forest is structured.

Bearing that in mind, and seeing how natural one's garden tends to become without one even having to think about it, it may well be worth looking deeper to see if there are other lessons that can be learnt from climatic climax forest vegetation and applied in the natural garden.

Two things stand out very clearly about climatic climax vegetation. The first is that all the space in the forest is used: the other is that there is a tremendous mixture of plant types and species. The forest floor is full of micro-flora and micro-fauna; there are bulbs in the soil and the floor of the forest itself is covered in a great diversity of ferns, grasses, orchids and woodland flowers. Then there are shrubs, small trees, the understorey trees, and finally the forest trees themselves. Very often vines climb and clamber over the ground and up through the trees, while in areas of high humidity many ferns and mosses grow as epiphytes on the branches of the trees. If you have a garden that is essentially woodland in character, try to utilize space the way plants do in a forest. Make sure that there are shade-bearing shrubs under the taller trees, and that in the clearings between them there are ferns, grasses, orchids and other plants that grow well in shade. Make use of your trees for growing vines – clematis, wisteria – they look so much better that way than tied onto poles.

A climatic climax forest is a self-sufficient ecological entity, almost entirely completely self-recycling. Leaf-fall from the trees is trapped by the shrubs and the ground level plants, so that little escapes. This lays down a natural mulch. A climatic climax forest is, however, pretty vast in terms of acreage, and it takes a pretty vast acreage for a woodland to become self-recycling. A woodland garden is not large enough to be self-supporting, let alone a woodland glade within a garden. It must be constantly mulched liberally with compost and bulky organic matter. Leaves that blow out of the woodland area should be swept up, stored in a bin, and applied as a mulch later, once they have rotted down sufficiently to prevent them from merely blowing away again. Make use of low-growing shrubs and carpeting plants, especially wintergreen ferns, as barriers round the edges of woodland glades to catch the natural leaf fall and prevent it from blowing away.

It would be a grave mistake to think that the only type of

ornamental garden is the woodland garden, or that only the best garden plants are essentially plants of open lands, of downlands, meadows, steppes and so on. This vegetation is mainly perennial, some of it annual. The leaf-fall is less obvious than in a forest: grasses, the dominant vegetation of many of these areas, keeps growing, forever re-cycling its own dead leaves as they rot and fall under the growing leaves. The activities of small animals and of earthworms and other micro-organisms ensure that the leaves that do fall do not remain in one place but are mixed with other leaves in the soil. The droppings of animals, which themselves have fed largely on the vegetation, also add humus to the soil.

The average garden, if there is such a thing, combines both types of vegetation, the forest type and the steppe or open plain type. Because of this, neither achieves any even semi-permanently balanced recycling. The plants in a garden, however densely they cover the soil, simply do not provide sufficient humus for everything to thrive. It is necessary to add and to keep adding plenty of bulky organic material. For one thing, a garden should always look more fertile than the land around it, and this is one way of achieving it. The other is to use napalm on the surrounding countryside.

One of the most noticeable things that both types of vegetation have in common is the enormous mixture of plant genera and species. Even in grasslands, where it is easy to think that all grasses are merely grasses, there are in fact highly complex populations of different species and different genera, and however much the grass may dominate grasslands, it is never the exclusive plant of the region: dozens, perhaps, hundreds, of other plants grow in happy association with them.

The moral is that you hardly ever find monoculture in nature, so do not try it in your own garden. The reason for saying that you hardly ever find it is that there are some plants which so dominate some areas that you might well think that some natural monoculture had occurred. Cattails, for example, often grow in great stands in the mud on pond-sides and river shallows. But there is a difference between this and a field of wheat or rice. Each wheat or rice plant is a single, individual plant. The cattails are simply one great clump of the same plant, often started from a single detached rhizome which has spread and sprawled through the mud to make the great stand. Bracken or brake often dominates areas of acid soil in a similar way. Yet even with these examples you will find, if you look closely, that other plants are closely packed between the dominant plant of the area. It is worth bearing in mind too, that very often these plants which naturally form great stands, are self-defeating. In time the cattails can block the water course in whose mud they once grew. They may even block it to the extent that the water no longer flows, or has to find some other course, in which case the cattails die out. Besides, they are colonizers of the mud, turning it into firm land in which true land plants, rather than marginals can grow.

Avoid monoculture is a prime rule in natural gardening. The more plants of the same genus or species you have growing together in one place, the more likely they are to be attacked by some bug specific to that plant. If you grow, for example, fifty rhododendrons together and one of them gets bud blast (fungal infection) it is far more likely that this will spread to the other forty-nine plants than if you have the same fifty rhododendrons interspersed with camellias, magnolias, maples, stewarties and eucryphias. The bugs that are specific to one plant will very often dislike the plant next door to it, and this will limit the spread of the bug. Besides, the plant next door may be the favourite breeding ground of the bug that preys on the bug that is specific to the plant you first thought of. And so on. A good garden, from the natural gardener's point of view, is one in which there is a rich mixture of plants from different stages of evolution, from the modest ferns to the highly developed grasses, from lilies to forget-me-nots, from pine to gum tree.

From the point of view of the health of the plants it helps too, if you can provide the most varied range of habitats you can create, even in a very small garden. You may have woodland and open land, but if you can have too some raised beds where sun-lovers can flourish under conditions of perfect drainage, but have too a bog garden, where you can grow the plants that enjoy those conditions your variety of plant life will be richer. Variation of habitat will do more than any other single thing to increase the range of plants you can grow. But only grow plants that will grow well in the conditions you can provide. If you want healthy plants in a healthy soil, do not attempt to grow bog plants unless you have an area where conditions are wet enough for them to flourish. By the same token, do not attempt to grow plants that need perfect drainage if you cannot provide such conditions. If you want to grow a rarity that needs very special cultural treatment, go to whatever lengths are necessary in order to provide those conditions: or do not try it at all. It is useless in a garden, where what you are after is every plant growing healthily, to put the whole lot at risk by struggling to keep alive one languishing rarity.

I have commented how in nature everything seems to strive to cover the soil completely. It is as though nature abhors bare earth. In fact it does not: it is simply that through evolution some plant has adapted itself to exploit almost every conceivable situation. In the ornamental garden one should strive too, to leave no earth uncovered. Where trees and shrubs are grown, ground cover plants should be grown under them. Where perennials are grown these should be planted sufficiently closely together to provide a green mantle over the soil. Where bedding schemes are used thick mulches should be used to suppress weeds while plants get established. If planted at their correct distances apart most bedding plants will completely cover the soil.

There are occasions where the use of ground-cover plants and the principles of ground cover is not always easy to apply. In new gardens for example where the soil is still being worked into a good condition, ground cover would impede this process. Further, the most efficient ground-cover plants are those that grow very densely, and these are usually rather slow to increase. Where you want to use effective ground cover the options are either to make do with something more coarse growing while you build up stocks, or else to mulch heavily with shredded or chipped pine bark, which lasts for a long time on the soil and is an effective suppressor of weeds.

Stone chippings can also provide an excellent form of ground cover, and are ideal where a minimum-maintenance garden is wanted. Use whatever stone chippings are most readily available in your area: most of the cost of such chippings is in the cost of transporting them. Work the soil well before you apply the chippings, and then apply them round the permanent plants in a layer about 7cm/3in deep, and apply a further layer every five years. Although this does little to enrich the soil such leaves as do fall on the soil will be readily washed or pulled down through the chippings, which themselves will keep the soil moisture level constant, which in turn encourages plenty of micro-organic activity in the soil.

Lastly, in the really natural garden, try to avoid harsh distinctions or divisions between the vegetable garden and the decorative garden. Mix potatoes and petunias: marigolds and beans. It may seem a strange idea at first, but try it: you will suddenly realize that many vegetables have a decorative value that you had never realised before. Apart from which both flowers and vegetables will grow better.

12 / The Rose Garden

Once upon not so very long ago there was a clergyman who liked roses. His name was the Reverend S. Reynolds Hole, Dean of Rochester. He liked them so much that he eventually became the founder of the British Royal National Rose Society. He had a vision of an England for ever beautified by roses, and it was he who said 'There should be beds of roses, banks of roses, bowers of roses, hedges of roses, vistas and alleys of roses.' And people believed him and launched upon the gardens of the civilized world one of the worst examples of decorative monoculture known to man. It is estimated that in Britain alone more than 50,000,000 rose plants are sold every year – one for every member of the population, adult, infant and senile. Though quite why the British should have taken up the cult of the rose with such a vengeance is difficult to understand when the British native species are so poor: the roses of the east and of America are vastly superior. Be that as it may, the British, the English in particular, have taken up the rose, and seem unlikely to relinquish it.

The problem is not that the rose is not a beautiful flower. It is. It is an extremely beautiful flower, even in its modern hybrid forms. If you were to come upon one suddenly, as it were unexpectedly, thrusting its perfectly shaped blossoms up among surrounding flowers of delphinium, pelargonium, asters and so on, you would marvel at its beauty. Grown in that way it will even stop in its tracks people who will walk past whole beds – indeed whole gardens, of nothing but roses *en masse* and *ad nauseam.*

From the point of view of anyone attempting to garden without chemicals, roses present two problems. The first is that they have been so highly cross-bred, inbred and overbred that they are probably prone to more diseases than any other ornamental plants: the other is that they are traditionally grown in beds on their own — a typical case of monoculture.

Roses, especially the modern hybrids, are prone to problems however you grow them and wherever you grow them. However, if you grow them just as you would grow any other shrub in a garden run without chemicals, you can minimize the number of problems they will suffer from, and also the amount of damage done by any particular pest. This really means growing roses, not in beds on their own, but dotted around the garden, among other shrubs, and perennial plants. The rather specialized pruning requirements of the modern hybrid roses however, make them unsuitable for planting in dense shrubberies, though the old-fashioned and species roses will thrive under such conditions. Because of their pruning needs modern roses are better grown among the perennial plants. Then, when the perennials are cut down to ground level in spring, the roses can easily be pruned at the same time. Modern practice happily works as well for roses as it does for perennial plants. Whereas the idea used to be to cut perennials to ground level in the fall, and clean the beds up at that time of year, modern practice is to shorten growths back, to remove unsightly seedheads and so on in the fall, but to leave the main cutting down till spring. The thinking behind this is largely that the stems left on the plants over winter help to protect the crowns and new buds from damage by winter frosts. With roses too, the practice is now to cut them back lightly in the fall, mainly to remove dead wood and to prevent long growths from causing windrock, and to do the major pruning work in the spring.

The advantage of growing roses in this way, apart from their probably looking better, is that if any disease settles on one rose plant it will not immediately move onto the next rose plant because there is nothing else available for it. Instead it will have to cross a barrier of many different plants, of different genera and species, before it can reach the next rose. Furthermore you are far more likely to be able to deal with an infestation on an isolated rose bush than you are when they are growing *en masse*.

If you must grow your modern hybrid roses in isolated beds, and some people still consider that it is the only 'proper' way to grow roses, then it is doubly essential that you work the soil into really good heart before planting the roses, and that you feed it annually and liberally with bulky organic materials. Hygiene will become particularly important: every dead twig must be removed the moment it is seen, and the roses should be inspected carefully at least once a week, preferably more frequently than that, during the growing season, not only for dead wood but for the first signs of an infestation. Only by doing this will you be able to spot a disease on one plant before all the roses in the bed become infected. Every dead leaf and fallen flower should be removed from the bushes and from the beds, for these provide a focal point for fungal infections which can virtually wipe out a whole bed of roses in a season or two.

Even if you want to grow your roses in a bed all on their own, there are still methods available to you to prevent this from becoming a total monoculture. It may become a duo-culture or even trio-culture, but even that is better than monoculture. Some sort of companion planting will help roses to remain free from pests and disease. If your soil is right you need not worry about mildew, so aphids will be your main problem. They are an important problem since they are widely believed to be the prime carriers of many of the other diseases that afflict roses. This being so, plainly whatever you can do to keep aphids away from your roses will be beneficial to you both.

One of the oldest of all known companion planting is roses and chives. It has been shown in controlled tests that where roses are growing in close association with chives they are vastly less likely to be attacked by aphids. Put another way: the chances of aphids attacking roses are between 85% and 90% higher where the roses are not growing in a bed of chives. It need not even be a whole bed to be effective. Even an edging of chives round the bed will prove effective.

Rather than having the traditional bare earth in the centre of the bed among the roses, plant something useful there. The reason for leaving the soil in the centre bare is because if you planted bedding plants, for example, they would be trampled to death in the course of your regular, routine maintenance of your roses. So plant something there that does not matter too much, preferably something that does not mind being walked on. Try chamomile, or thyme. You can make attractive patterns under the roses by planting chives, thyme and chamomile together, or by using the green form of thyme together with the yellow-leaved form, or with one of the variegated forms.

If you are growing roses without chemicals it is worth taking one last look at nature. Walk through a field or forest and count the number of perfect plants you see. If you look closely you will find that almost every plant has a leaf that has been nibbled here, a caterpillar on it there, an egg-cluster lurking under a leaf somewhere else. Plants are never totally perfect in the wild. Do not expect them to be totally perfect in your garden either, for that is to expect the impossible from them. Especially if, as is usual with roses, you are growing many of the same type of plant in close association with each other.

13/Lawns

A lawn stands in very much the same relationship to a garden as a pair of shoes does to a suit. It does not matter how smart your suit, it will look dreadful if you are wearing dirty, scruffy shoes. Put on some smartly polished shoes, and the suit will appear in its true colours. The same goes for lawns. No matter how beautiful your garden, it will never look really good unless you have a rich green beautifully mown lawn to show it off.

Anyone who has seen the lawns of the Colleges at Oxford or Cambridge has a pretty clear idea in their mind what a good lawn should look like. A rich American is reputed once to have so much wanted a lawn as beautiful as these that he asked one of the men tending the lawns what he would have to do to his lawn in order for it to look as good as that. He was told that he would have to lay it flat and level, in ground well prepared, that he would have to take out every weed by hand, that he would have to roll it and spike it and feed it, rake out the moss and mow it three times a week from spring till autumn, and that he would have to keep on doing this for three hundred years.

The truth is that that really is what you have to do if you want a lawn that will look good and feel good to walk on. Modern chemicals seem to have offered a short cut: it is possible by the use of modern chemicals to achieve a weedfree lawn of vivid greenness in just a year or two. Which may save you 288 years hard work. The problem is that the usual ingredient of lawn feeds that kills the weeds is 2,4-D. It does not just kill the weeds. It kills the worms and the birds that feed on the worms. And that vivid greenness is just a drug-induced hallucination. The lawn is literally living in a drugged state of euphoria. Withdraw the heavy application of chemicals, and the withdrawal symptoms will be almost immediately noticeable.

Such a lawn is obviously out of the question for anyone attempting to garden without chemicals. But to deny yourself the use of chemicals does not mean that your lawn need look any the worse for it. Indeed, if you treat it well, it will probably look rather better for it.

The first thing to be appreciated about a lawn is that it is not a carpet. If you want a carpet, buy one. They make very good plastic lawns these days. All you have to do is water them. You have to water them because they build up so much static electricity that they collect all the dust from miles around.

A lawn is a multitude of living plants. There are literally millions of grass plants in any lawn. Curiously, a lawn is not quite a monoculture, though it may seem it, because in any good lawn there is a complex mixture of grasses involving several species and genera. Each of those millions of lawn plants has just the same cultural and nutritional requirements as your most prized specimen plant. Each one needs air and water at the roots, a soil rich in organic matter, and freedom from competition by weeds. Appreciate that one simple fact and you can probably work out what you need to do in order to have a lawn that looks good and feels good for yourself.

If you are starting a lawn from scratch, prepare the soil thoroughly, digging it well and incorporating plenty of bulky organic materials. Leave it a year and allow it to settle, then lightly rake over the surface. Add a last dressing of finely sifted compost, and then either seed (choosing a seed well suited to your soil and situation) or turf it, again choosing a turf compatible with your soil. The finest lawns are usually made on neutral or slightly alkaline soils, and you may consider it worth correcting your pH if it is acid or exceptionally alkaline.

Once the lawn is established it should be mown regularly, preferably one way one time and cross-ways the next time. The first mowing should be made as early in the year as possible, just as soon as the ground is dry enough to use the mower. The blades should be set quite high for the first and last mowings of the year, but a closer cut can be achieved through the summer months. The last mow of the season is important too: do not stop mowing till the lawn stops growing. Most people only have time to mow their lawns once a week, but for perfection it should be mown as much as three times a week in high summer.

Mowing does several things to the lawn. It stimulates the grass plants to grow, and since they cannot grow upwards (every time they try to grow upwards this wretched machine comes over them again and takes their tops off) they grow outwards, forming ever more and more dense mats. Which is just what you want in a lawn. Grasses that have matted closely together give weeds little chance of surviving, usually little chance of germinating. Even if they do germinate the mowing machine takes the seed-leaves off, and very few plants can survive when that happens.

But you do something else when you mow your lawn: you take something out of the natural cycle of growth, death and re-use. In meadow land dead grass leaves just rot down among the roots of the grass: when you mow a lawn you remove these clippings in the hopper. Do not make the mistake of mowing without the hopper in the belief that the clippings will feed the lawn where they fall: they won't. They will simply clog it up. But you do have to replace the goodness you take away every time you mow the lawn.

The way to do this is to top dress the lawn regularly, preferably spring and fall, but sometimes a light dressing in high summer is useful, particularly if you live on a sandy, fast-draining soil. The finest material you can use for feeding your lawn is garden compost that has rotted till it has the consistency of moss peat. Sift this into very fine particles, then top dress the whole lawn, either by hand or using a mechanical spreader. Basic slag, bonfire ash and sedge peat are also good materials for top dressing a lawn. The important thing, whichever of these materials you use, is to use them regularly.

Mowing does something else to lawns too: it compacts them. Since the grass plants need both air and water at their roots, you need to aerate the lawn to compensate for the compression caused not only by the mower but by people walking over the grass. You can aerate a lawn either by spiking it systematically with a garden fork, or by using a spiking tool designed for the purpose.

All weeds should be removed by hand. A daisy fork is a useful tool, not only for getting out the daises, but also for removing a great many other weeds. Deep rooted weeds like dandelions can either be dug up with a fork, which will temporarily make quite a mess of the lawn, or killed by applying table salt to the crown. The salt should be applied at the rate of about half a teaspoonful right in the centre of the plant while it is in vigorous growth. Do not over do the salt though, it is poisonous to quite a lot of plants so you do not want too much of it accumulating in the soil. Used this way it will usually be perfectly all right.

Moss is another weed which needs to be dealt with. Though its presence can give a lawn a pleasant, springy feel underfoot, it will in time smother the grass plants. If you want a moss lawn, make a moss lawn. But if you want a conventional all-grass lawn, get rid of the moss. The mere fact that moss has appeared in a lawn usually points to bad drainage. The real way to get rid of moss is to improve the drainage. However, in high rainfall areas, moss will appear in lawns even where the drainage is good. The remedy is to rake it out, using a fine toothed wire rake. Moss has no roots, only radicles which serve to draw water up from the soil, so it will come away from the ground very easily.

The lawn should be raked annually with a fine-toothed wire rake to clear any clippings that have fallen between the plants. The hopper usually lets quite a high proportion fall. A normal, healthy lawn should only need raking once a year, preferably in autumn, after the last mowing, and should then be given a top dressing.

Worm casts on a lawn can look unsightly. This has led generations of gardeners to kill the worms with all sorts of lethal substances. The answer is not to kill the worms, rather to encourage them. The casts show that there is an active worm population under your lawn, helping micro-organisms to flourish, creating humus, mixing your top dressings into the soil at a level where the roots of the grass can use it. The time to start worrying is when you do not have any worm casts on your lawn.

If you treat the individual plants in your lawn with the same care and consideration that you would give to any other plants in your garden, it will not only look better than the chemically drugged lawns of your neighbours, it will last longer too, and be a very eloquent reminder to yourself and your friends that it is possible to garden successfully without chemicals.

14 / Looking Ahead

We all like to succeed at whatever we are doing, and the dream or promise of instant success appeals to most of us even more than the dream of hard-won success. Perhaps the greatest of the temptations offered by the modern lethal pesticides, insecticides, miticides and herbicides available today is that they do seem to promise instant success. The whole marketing strategy of the companies manufacturing these chemicals seems to be designed deliberately to implant into your mind and mine the idea that we can be rid of almost any garden nuisance, instantly, at the squirt of an aerosol. The success of these modern chemicals in killing bugs may indeed be instant – but it is also illusory. The undesirable ecological repercussions of that instant success may take years, even decades, to cure or, in some cases, even to become apparent.

The truth is that in no field of human endeavour is success ever instant. Were it to be so, it would not be worth having. Success of any type is something that can only be achieved by working for it, by discipline and by having in one's mind's eye a clear image of just what it is that one is striving for.

Natural gardening is no recipe for instant success. It is a recipe for success in the long run, a permanent achievement. Indeed, in the short term, its effects may even be counter-productive. It is worth bearing in mind that if you have been using chemicals in your garden regularly, even for quite a short time, or if you have taken over a garden in which chemicals have been used for a long time, you may well, when you decide to kick the chemical killer habit, find a 'bug rebound' phenomenon. The bugs have, after all, been chemically repressed: suddenly released from their drugged repression they will re-assert themselves with vigour, just as someone who has had symptoms of acute anxiety repressed by a sedative will, if the drug is withdrawn prematurely, break out in a violent attack of those symptoms.

Fear not. The 'bug rebound' is a short-lived phenomenon. It may create havoc in your garden for a year, but after that you will find your garden moving forward, the bugs gradually moving into a precarious balance with themselves. There is a very simple reason for the short-lived period of the 'bug rebound'. Two things happen when you withdraw the chemicals from the garden. The first is that the undesirable bugs increase in numbers: the second is that their predators increase in numbers. But beyond the way the beneficial bugs are increasing in numbers to help you something else is happening: the undesirable bugs, having eaten their way through all they can find, start to run out of food. Many will die of starvation: others will migrate. Both ways, their numbers will start to diminish, probably by the end of your first summer without chemicals.

However, to be sure of success, and in natural gardening terms this brings us back to the basic proposition of a healthy plant in a healthy soil, you need to do everything you can to improve your soil structure and its humus content throughout that first year. The gains you make in your first year, if you really work hard at it, will be far more dramatic than you are likely to believe until you try it. They are almost as dramatic as the increase in crop yields achieved by some very dangerous chemicals. The difference is that, whereas with chemicals the gains made in year one are huge, the gains made in successive years are relatively small: by improving your soil year by year you gain more year by year. You never actually reach the point at which you cannot increase the productivity of your garden by keeping working on the soil.

But over and above anything you may have learned from this book, keep your ears and eyes open, keep your mind open, to new ideas and new techniques of natural gardening. There are advances being made all the time: some of them may be worthwhile, others may prove dangerous in ways we have not even thought of yet. There are, for example, almost continuous experiments going on into companion plantings, and it is being found that more and more plants deter more and more insects, and that particular combinations are proving more successful than others. There is increasing evidence that repellent plantings really work, and the list of repellent plants is an ever-increasing one. What are known as trap crops are being intensively investigated at the moment: the idea of trap crops is that the enemy bugs like them so much they stay to eat them instead of moving on to the plants that you want to eat or otherwise enjoy. The problem with some of these ideas is that, although it may keep your garden bugs under control, it may also mean that you find yourself growing plants that you would not otherwise consider worthy of garden space. If success of any sort is to be achieved, sacrifices have to be made, and this is perhaps the only sacrifice you may have to make in order to succeed at natural gardening. It is a very small price to pay compared with the dangers of the chemical alternative.

Other more dramatic but very promising new avenues are being explored. One is to kill the enemy bugs in your garden by introducing into their populations bugs of the same type that have been infected by viruses which will in one way or another reduce the bug populations by making them sick. These microbial pathogens can work in several ways: they may kill the bugs outright, or they may affect their reproductive cycle, make them sterile, or prevent them getting beyond the juvenile stage of their development. In cases where the microbial pathogens do not kill the bugs outright they almost certainly make them easier prey for other controls and diseases. This work is still very much in the experimental stage, and it may be that there is a danger that the microbial pathogens could be passed on from the enemy bugs to the beneficial bugs. However, one fundamental difference exists in the attitudes of the scientists working on controls of this type and those workings on the development of chemicals of the more dangerous types: the people doing this work have a genuine and sincere concern for the interrelationships of living things, and they are unlikely to unleash these microbial pathogens onto the market until they have been fully and extensively tested and proven.

Another promising line of control is the use of auxins. It is known that different auxins are produced in the bodies of all insects at different periods of their life-cycle: one auxin tells the insect when to moult, when to pupate, when to reproduce and so on. By using insecticides that are quite simply synthetic auxins it is possible, for example, to prevent them from ever getting further than their juvenile stage – in which case they never reach the age at which they can reproduce. The only problem with this type of approach is that, in time, it would tend to rob the beneficial insects of their natural prey and so cause a decline in their numbers. However, there might well be a case for using techniques of this type in epidemic situations to help to restore something approaching a balance between enemy bugs and beneficial bugs. Again, research here is still experimental.

Overall the emphasis of all the new research reveals a new attitude. Research workers talk now of 'control' – not as they did until very recently of eradication, and this is true both of bugs and weeds. And it has taken a very long time for this change of attitude to come about.

It is worth remembering that it is as long ago as 1962 that Rachel Carson published her mind-opening book *The Silent Spring* – that eerie story of a town in America to which the spring did not come: leaves unfurled, blossoms opened, but no birds sang, no bees buzzed among the flowers, and the farm animals produced no young.

Two years after the publication of that book farmers in the United States of America used 65,000,000kg/143,000,000lbs of insecticides. In 1970 over 226,750,000kg/500,000,000lbs of insecticides were used. There has been a parallel increase in the amount of chemical fertilizer used in the United Kingdom. The point here is that in year one you may use the fertilizer at the recommended rate and achieve, for example, a 100% increase in yield. In year two, for the same dosage, you achieve only 10-15% increase on top of that. By year five, even with double the rate of application, you can only increase your yield by perhaps one or two per cent.

The people who believe in chemicals as the ultimate solution to all gardening and agricultural problems, especially those of increasing yields, are likely to confront you with the question, with x,000,000 people dying of starvation every year, how can you justify abandoning chemical controls? The answer is twofold. In the first place, the actual yields of edible produce will increase rather than diminish once you adopt natural gardening attitudes and techniques. The other is that there is a world of difference between the intensive monoculture necessary in the growing of wheat or rice, and the mixed cropping in a home garden. It is that mixture that makes natural gardening so easy, so successful, and natural farming so very much more difficult.

The great thing with natural gardening is that once you start yourself on that course, you must never look back, not even once. There can be no going back, no reaching for a chlorinated hydrocarbon aerosol simply because something seems to have got out of hand. One shot of that and you will undo so much of what you have achieved that it simply is not worth while. There is no halfway between natural gardening and chemical gardening. Either you practice natural gardening, or you do not. You cannot practice natural gardening on your vegetables, but not on your lawn or your roses. If you find that year after year your favourite rose gets black spot, do not weaken, do not resort to chemicals. Find a rose resistant to black spot. That is the true attitude of the natural gardener.

If anyone tries to mock you by telling you that natural gardening is a retrogressive step, an ostrich-in-the-sand attitude, and that it is wrong to reject all that our sophisticated industrio-technological civilization can offer, just persuade them to compare your natural garden with their unnatural garden. Point out to them the dark rich soil you have created, show them how healthy all the plants are, how tasty the fruits and vegetables are and point out to them that you are working with nature, not against it.

There are only two prerequisites for success in natural gardening: firstly you must believe in it, and secondly you must persevere in your belief. You must get the soil structure right, then persevere with making compost and mulching with it, persevere in using barrier plantings and trap plantings, persevere in using disease resistant varieties of the plants you want to grow, persevere in avoiding monoculture and seeking new ways of creating workable companion plantings, persevere in ruthlessly weeding out weak or sickly plants and resolutely resist the temptation to backslide into the use of chemicals in the garden.

The one thing that most seems to impress the people who visit the game parks in Africa more than anything else is that you never see a sick animal. You never, for example, see a sickly zebra: all the zebra are sleek coated and well-fed. There are no sick zebra because the lions and the hyenas and the jackals and the vultures have disposed of them. The natural garden presents much the same aspect: there are no sickly plants there, only an aspect of a garden full of healthy plants thriving in a healthy soil. It is a reward worth working for.

Appendix / **Dangerous Chemicals**

There are two groups of synthetic insecticides which are so dangerous they should never be used in any garden at all. If, under epidemic conditions and only under epidemic conditions, you have to resort to using an insecticide at all, use one of those recommended in this book, based on naturally occurring insecticides found in many plants, or use milk, vegetable oil or some similar harmless remedy.

Group 1: Chlorinated hydrocarbons.
This is by far the most dangerous of the two groups of synthetic insecticides. It includes such compounds as DDT, benzene hex-achloride (BHC – which is now often recommended as a 'safe' alternative to DDT), dieldrin, aldrin, lindane, chlordane, isodrin, toxophene and several similar products, some of them simply combinations of some of those listed above.

DDT is by far the most thoroughly studied of the chlorinated hydrocarbons, and most of these comments concerning this group of insecticides are based on researches with DDT. Other chlori-nated hydrocarbons vary in their generally higher degree of solubility in water, their greater toxicity and in that they are generally slightly less persistent.

Chlorinated hydrocarbons are broad-spectrum poisons. They work primarily on the central nervous system, although the pre-cise ways in which they work are not yet clearly understood. The effects of chlorinated-hydrocarbon poisoning range from hyper-excitability to death following violent convulsions and paralysis. Insects are far more readily affected by these compounds than almost any other group of creatures because these insecticides are more readily absorbed by the insect cuticle than, for example, by the mammalian skin. However, fish and other aquatic animals are particularly sensitive to chlorinated-hydrocarbon poisoning. It seems that these compounds work on fish by blocking the oxygen uptake at the gills, with the result that the fish die of suffocation. Although again the actual mechanics of why this happens are not yet well understood, it is well established that it does happen. Chlorinated hydrocarbons can apparently induce the production of enzymes (chemicals which govern body functions) and it is most probably this that accounts for the widely differing effects of this group of poisons on different creatures.

On man and other vertebrates – including domestic pets – this group of chemicals works in an insidious way, slowly accumulating in the fatty tissues of the body. The organs most often affected are the reproductive organs, the fatty tissues of the heart and the liver: in the last two cases substantial accumulations can be fatal. There is also increasing evidence that DDT in particular can cause cerebral haemorrhage and softening of the brain.

One of the ironies of the chlorinated hydrocarbons is that, while they are used to kill insects and so protect plants, they do in fact damage plants. Different hydrocarbons vary greatly in their toxicity to plants, and different plants vary in their sensitivity to chlorinated hydrocarbons. In most plants these compounds slow down the rate of photosynthesis: that in turn slows down the plant's rate of growth and output. It weakens the plant, making it less healthy and more susceptible to attack by insects and diseases. Again, it would seem to be the way in which chlorinated hydrocarbons accumulate in fatty tissues that causes this reduction in photosynthetic efficiency. Plant cell membranes, especially those concerned with photosynthesis, have a high fat content, and it is almost certainly these cells that malfunction under the impact of chlorinated hydrocarbons.

Beyond these considerations, there are four properties of all chlorinated hydrocarbons which make them, quite literally, a menace to mankind.

1) They are broad-spectrum poisons with a very wide range of biological activity.

2) They tend to gravitate towards that which is living as op-

posed to that which is inert. If you think of the world as being made up of two components — that which is living and that which is not — then the chlorinated hydrocarbons may be said to be continually moving from that which is not living into that which is living. The classic example of this is Clear Lake, California, mentioned in the introduction. This was sprayed with a chlorinated hydrocarbon, then tested to find out what concentration of that compound remained in the water two weeks later. It was found that there was no trace of the compound in the water. It had all been absorbed by the animals and other organisms living in the lake. Hence the hopelessness of trying to monitor DDT levels by testing the levels in drinking water.

3) Chlorinated hydrocarbons have great mobility. They combine readily with dust particles, and are blown literally all over the world. Similarly, DDT co-distills with water, so that when that water evaporates and is carried into the atmosphere, the DDT goes with it. Because of this property of mobility quite high concentrations of DDT have been found in parts of the world thousands of miles away from the nearest place it has been used.

4) Chlorinated hydrocarbons have great stability. It is known that 50% of a single spraying with DDT will still be found in the soil more than ten years later. The tragedy is that this does not mean that the other 50% has become biologically inactive: the probability is that it has been leached away by rainfall, ground seepage or consumption by some living creature. Even more tragic is the accumulating body of evidence to suggest that DDE, which is the biologically degraded form of DDT — ie. what DDT becomes once it is absorbed into your system — may be virtually immortal.

If any one of these factors was absent from the permutation the effects of chlorinated hydrocarbons would be much less frightening. For example, if it degenerated into biologically inactive molecules very rapidly, many of the problems created by these compounds could be resolved simply by banning them and waiting for the damage they have done to repair itself. If they were less mobile, the damage they do could be contained; and so on. There can be little doubt that if Machiavelli had really wanted to destroy the world, he would have invented chlorinated hydrocarbons.

Group 2: Organophosphates.

This group of insecticides have been developed from the lethal nerve gas Tabun (diisopropylfluorophosphate). That nerve gas was designed to kill people, not insects. The main insecticides developed from it are malathion, parathion, diazinon, azodrin, TEPP, phosdrin and several others: many are sold in combination either with other compounds of the same group, or with chlorinated hydrocarbons.

All these compounds work on the same principle: they are all cholinesterase inhibitors. What that means is that they inactivate the enzyme responsible for breaking down a nerve transmitter substance – acetylcholine. Once this nerve transmitter substance has been broken down, the nervous system runs wild, responding to every nerve message transmitted by the brain. The whole central nervous system becomes hyperactive, and insects and animals die twitching and totally out of control. However hideous death by organophosphate poisoning may be, unlike the chlorinated hydrocarbons, these compounds are short-lived and do not accumulate in the body. Consequently they do not cause long-term damage to the ecosystem.

Although the organophosphates are widely regarded as being far less dangerous to man than the chlorinated hydrocarbons, there is a fallacy here. In fact, they are extremely dangerous to all mammals. The reason they kill insects so readily is that the nerve transmitter enzyme which they destroy is far more critical to the functioning of an insect than it is in man.

The hidden danger is that these organophosphates inhibit other enzymes in mammals besides acetylcholine. For example, malathion, which is extremely poisonous to insects, is relatively, but only relatively, harmless to man because the human system contains an enzyme, carboxy-esteraze, which destroys the malathion. However, some of the other organophosphates destroy the carboxy-esteraze: the human body will then have no safeguard against the malathion, and acute malathion poisoning could follow. Thus if you were to eat for a main course a salad which contained lettuce which had been sprayed with an organophosphate which destroyed the carboxy-esteraze in your system, and were to conclude your meal with an apple sprayed with malathion, the combination could be fatal.

It is a risk not worth running.

Apart from these insecticides, ALL herbicides should be regarded as extremely poisonous.

Index

ALUN CHALFONT
Montgomery of Alamein

'Monty' – The Field Marshal Viscount Montgomery of Alamein – is a household name, especially for those who lived through the Second World War. His victories in the Western Desert earned him an international reputation as one of the greatest soldiers of his day. Montgomery was also one of the greatest paradoxes of recent military history – a general loved by his soldiers, feared by his enemies and heartily disliked by many of his contemporaries.

Alun Chalfont's concern in this biography is not so much to analyse Montgomery's campaigns in depth, but rather to discover 'Monty', the man behind the famous battles.

'Unquestionably the best study'   *Sunday Telegraph*

'I found myself enthralled'   *Daily Telegraph*

H. MONTGOMERY HYDE
Oscar Wilde

Oscar Wilde's wit continues to delight readers and audiences all over the globe, and the drama of his life remains one of the really astonishing and moving true stories in the world of letters. This is the most complete biography to date, with new information which has come to light in recent years; and it is the most outspoken about his homosexual affairs.

'A biography that is thorough, fair, immensely readable'
          Anthony Powell, Daily Telegraph

DAVID DUFF
Elizabeth of Glamis

Queen Elizabeth the Queen Mother is one of the most outstanding and best-loved personalities of our time. This magnificent biography presents a fascinating study of her public career, including her war-time efforts, the numerous visits to Australia, New Zealand, Canada and the United States, and the tireless support she gave her husband King George VI and later her daughter Queen Elizabeth II. It also takes an intensely human look at her more private life and interests from childhood onwards.

J. J. SCARISBRICK
Henry VIII

Henry VIII's flamboyant and forceful personality dominated his age and has never lost its fascination. Here Professor Scarisbrick writes with an eloquence and authority worthy of the importance of his subject and his book has become the standard life of Henry VIII.

'This book is a triumph of biography consonant with the interest and importance of its theme'
Glanmor Williams, New Statesman

'A book which no teacher of the period can safely neglect'
The Times Educational Supplement

BRIAN GARDNER
Up the Line to Death

The War Poets 1914–1918

Before his death on active service in 1918 Wilfred Owen had written, 'Above all I am not concerned with Poetry. My subject is War and the pity of War.' This anthology, too, is concerned more with the First World War than with poetry; it is not only a collection, but a book with a theme. Seventy-two poets are represented, of whom twenty-one died in action.

Kipling, Brooke, Sassoon, Blunden, Owen are all here, as well as poets almost entirely forgotten now. From the early exultation to the bitter disillusion, the tragedy of the First World War is carefully traced in the words of those who lived through it.

'Mr Brian Gardner, who has chosen, introduced and put notes to this admirable anthology, shows the First World War poets in all moods.'   *The Times*

'To read through this anthology . . . is to live the years 1914–18, adding, to the images of battle which most of us have already the actual feelings expressed by the soldier poets who lived, and died, through trench warfare.'
                    The Times Educational Supplement

The Terrible Rain

The War Poets 1939–1945

This is a companion volume to Brian Gardner's anthology of the poetry of the First World War, *Up the Line to Death*. Many of the poets of the Second World War – at least forty of whom died on active service – are already forgotten. But here, too, are the poets whose fame has endured: Keith Douglas, Sidney Keyes, Alun Lewis, and John Pudney; and the poets of the 'Home Front' like Louis MacNeice and Dylan Thomas.

Over thirty years later these poems can be seen to be remarkable in their faithful recording of the spirit of their time. Anyone who remembers the Second World War will find in these pages the accurate and moving evocation of an age.

JOHN BRAINE
Life at the Top

Joe Lampton is a success – or so it seems. He's married to a rich man's daughter, has a well-paid job, and now belongs to the wealthy class he used to envy. But after ten years of affluent living he faces a crisis in his life. Once again his restless drive towards other women and material success begins to assert itself, and Joe is ready to break out . . .

The Pious Agent

Introducing Xavier Flynn, fervent Catholic and ruthless professional killer. The enemy is FIST, a secret revolutionary group – their mission is sabotage, their target one of Britain's best-established industries. Grappling with a ferment of intrigue, counter-plotting and violent death demands the ultimate degree of razor-sharp wits and ice-cool experience. But Xavier is a born survivor – with one eye fixed on heaven and the other on the nearest desirable woman.

'Mr Braine is a highly welcome newcomer to the spy story scene.'
Francis Goff, *Sunday Telegraph*

The Jealous God

Vincent Dungarvan is a young schoolmaster, thirty years old but still a virgin. His mother wishes him to become a Roman Catholic priest, and he himself half believes he has the vocation. Then he meets Laura – erotically attractive as well as intelligent, open and warm. He passionately wants to marry her, but his church stands as a barrier between them . . .

J. I. M. STEWART
The Gaudy

The first novel in his Oxford quintet.

On the occasion of an annual dinner, Duncan Pattullo revisits his Oxford college for the first time in many years. He meets again old friends and enemies of his undergraduate days, and as the evening passes he finds himself increasingly involved in a series of extraordinary developments that bring him closer to the new Oxford generation as well as his own.

Young Pattullo

The second novel in his Oxford quintet.

Arriving for his first term at Oxford, the youthful Duncan Pattullo encounters the mixed collection of undergraduates who will become his friends. Characteristic Oxford rumpuses and calamities help bring together the tenants of his college staircase in incidents of unpredictable comedy blended with wry nostalgia. This is a story of the Oxford of earlier days, now gone for ever, but here recalled with deep affection.

A Memorial Service

The third novel in his Oxford quintet.

Duncan Pattullo returns in middle age to take up a fellowship at his old college. He finds the Provost, Dr Pococke, much concerned to secure a huge benefaction from a charitable trust likely to be influenced by the aged and often outrageous Cedric Mumford. The bad behaviour in college of Ivo Mumford, Cedric's luckless grandson, is very much a complicating factor – and becomes still more so when his forthcoming magazine, *Priapus*, proves even more objectionable than its title suggests.

KEN KESEY
Sometimes a Great Notion

His brilliant successor to *One Flew over the Cuckoo's Nest*.

Hank Stamper has lived beside and fought with the Wakonda River in the State of Oregon all his life. The riverside house built by his father, old Henry, has become a fortress – both against the river, which after long years of erosion now swirls round three sides of it, and against the jealousies and rivalries of men. When Hank's college-educated half-brother Leland returns to his childhood home, in response to a cryptic summons, he is not sure whether Hank needs his help for the family logging business or simply wants to give him a further taste of the humiliation he knew there as a boy. In learning the answer to these questions he becomes involved in the Stamper clan's bitter battle with the union, the town and the forces of nature.

'The author's vitality is apparently boundless . . . His book is a brilliant performance'   *The Times*

'Raw American power . . . proud, stubborn, scornful, defiant'   *Playboy*

'As big and brawling as the country it describes'   *Time*

RONALD LOCKLEY
Seal Woman

Cut off by a high rampart of cliffs, the forgotten shoreline of Kilcalla Bay is filled with all the wild beauties of untouched nature. There a young stranger meets and falls in love with Shian, the seal girl, whose past is strangely interwoven with age-old legends about human ties with the inhabitants of the deep. As their relationship develops he decides he will accompany her when she swims with the seals to their refuge far out on the western horizon.

MONICA FURLONG
The Cat's Eye

For Bridget Reilly the invitation to spend the summer in Cornwall offers welcome relief from the pain of her marriage breaking up. Her hostess, Nell Wilbraham, is a strikingly beautiful woman, and when Bridget meets the rest of the family she is equally impressed. Another guest is the mysterious Paulinus, a good-looking and charming drifter who entrances them all with his almost pagan vitality. As the weeks pass, these people seem to take on a more vivid, magical quality which arouses in Bridget entirely new emotions and longings.

'This is a most enjoyable novel ... the book leaves one with a sense of having lived, for a while, among enriching company'   *Sunday Times*

'Her description of sterile marriage is superb. This is powerful prose'   *Cosmopolitan*

More top non-fiction available in Magnum

ALUN CHALFONT
417 0191   Montgomery of Alamein   £1.25

DAVID DUFF
417 0201   Elizabeth of Glamis   £1.25

BRIAN GARDNER
417 0235   Up the Line to Death   85p
417 0207   The Terrible Rain   85p

H. MONTGOMERY HYDE
417 0193   Oscar Wilde   £1.50

DAVE LAING
413 3186   The Electric Muse   75p

McRAE/CAIRNCROSS
417 0162   Capital City   85p
413 3344   The Second Great Crash   50p

J. J. SCARISBRICK
413 3368   Henry VIII   £1.50

These and other Magnum Books are available at your bookshop or newsagent.
In case of difficulties orders may be sent to:

Magnum Books
Cash Sales Department
PO Box 11
Falmouth
Cornwall TR1O 109EN

Please send cheque or postal order, no currency, for purchase price quoted
and allow the following for postage and packing:

UK   19p for the first book plus 9p per copy for each additional book
           ordered, to a maximum of 73p.

BFPO   19p for the first book plus 9p per copy for the next 6 books,
& Eire   thereafter 3p per book.

Overseas   20p for the first book and 10p per copy for each additional book.
customers

While every effort is made to keep prices low, it is sometimes necessary to
increase prices at short notice. Magnum Books reserve the right to show new
retail prices on covers which may differ from those previously advertised in
the text or elsewhere.